Controversies in Feminist Theology

Controversies in Contextual Theology Series

Controversies in Feminist Theology

Marcella Maria Althaus-Reid
and
Lisa Isherwood

scm press

© Marcella Maria Althaus-Reid and Lisa Isherwood 2007

The Authors have asserted their right under the Copyright, Designs
and Patents Act, 1988, to be identified as the Authors of this Work

British Library Cataloguing in Publication data

A catalogue record for this book is available
from the British Library

978 0 334 04050 7

First published in 2007 by SCM Press
9–17 St Alban's Place,
London N1 0NX

www.scm-canterburypress.co.uk

SCM Press is a division of
SCM-Canterbury Press Ltd

Typeset by Regent Typesetting, London
Printed and bound in Great Britain by
William Clowes Ltd, Beccles, Suffolk

Contents

Series Introduction   vii

Introduction   On Theology, Sisterhood and
                Controversies   1

1   Gender and Sexuality   17

2   Myths Surrounding Feminist Theological
    Hermeneutics   38

3   The Virgin Mary: Many Images, Many Interests   63

4   Christology   81

5   Life After Death   106

6   Controversies on the Future of Feminist Theologies   125

Bibliography   136

Index of Names and Subjects   142

Controversies in Contextual Theology

Contextual theologies such as Liberation, Black or Feminist theologies have been the object of critical studies in the past. Such critiques, especially when mounted by western academics, have tended to adopt an essentialist approach to these distinct theologies, assuming homogeneity in their development. In reality, on closer inspection, they display profound differences of both content and method. Controversies in Contextual Theology is the first series to highlight and examine these divisions. Each volume brings together two protagonists from within one form of contextual theology. The issues which divide them are openly addressed. Arguments are developed and positions clarified, but there is no guarantee that reconciliation can be achieved.

Marcella Althaus-Reid
Lisa Isherwood
Series editors

Introduction

On Theology, Sisterhood and Controversies

Feminist theology has come a long way in a short time as perhaps signalled by the plural in the title these days – theologies. Although we are using the term theologies here you will notice that we do not mention theology, this is because we are both Christian theologians and feel that any controversies that may exist within theology are best considered by one who is part of the debate in a more direct way than we are. Despite our caution in this matter we do feel that the maturity of the feminist theology movement is shown in the writing of this book, that is to say we are, at this early stage of development publically displaying some of the many controversies in key areas of feminist theologies. The uniqueness of this as a feminist undertaking is that we are not here to debunk the claims of others who may not hold the same position as ours, but rather to lay before the reader the full richness of this debate. One of the strengths of feminist theologies has always been the ability to include many voices within the debate. Of course detractors have seen this as a weakness, claiming that it signals a lack of internal methodological cohesion – as Mary Daly warned us years ago masculinist theology bows down to methodolatry and we should not do the same. This is not the same thing at all as having no method and no cohesion, it is however about creating space for diverse voices to express what they experience of the divine among and between us. It is about respect and an overwhelming belief that the divine cannot be contained by any one group whoever they may be and however blessed and sanctioned they believe themselves to be.

1

As a democratic movement feminist theology has to acknowledge that we will not all see things the same way and the task is finding a way to honour the difference. Further, it is at times very hard knowledge that those things we hold dear and in truth as almost self-evident will also be under question and open to critique and change. What feminist theologies offer, when we get it right, are a political challenge to a world that believes, or large parts seem to, that democracy once decided on can be exported with bombs and repression for the good of all. Freedom through death is a concept feminist theologies gave up a long time ago! For feminist theologies, democracy means that controversy will remain at the heart of what we do and that it will fuel us to greater engagement with a world in need of our passion. Our ability to live with disunity is our greatest strength and our greatest question remains how to have the disputes, not whether to have them.

Feminists have always been brave women; they have and do put their lives on the line for the debate to be opened or to continue. Most of us are never asked to actually lay down our lives but we do have to show bravery in the way in which we continue to question and not hide behind either moral certainty or the morality that calls some not to offend the many. We need to be brave in continually questioning our own thoughts and keeping those too open to the unfolding future; a future that 'takes place every time a possibility is imagined, a collective self reflection takes place, a dispute over values, priorities and language emerges'.[1] And of course those of us in the academy need to always remember that this is not an ivory tower debate and the outcomes are not simply nice conclusions on a page or in a report. Feminist theologies arise from the lives of all women and are aimed at expanding those lives through justice-seeking and right-relation, this is an embodied activity which loses all credibility when confined to the page.

We have travelled light years from a rather crude beginning in which we believed that we could and should define 'woman' to a

---

1 Judith Butler, *Undoing Gender*, New York: Routledge, 2004.

place of understanding, for the moment, that gender is far more flexible then that and that woman has many colours, ethnic origins, economic realities, religious feelings, social situations and sexual orientations. The woman at the heart of feminist theologies does not exist, yet she is everywhere and complex. The exploration of her complexity and the honouring of the findings are what give rise to the controversies in feminist theologies and this is where the uniqueness of this approach lies. It is in the delighted and joy-filled continued unfolding of the nature of woman and the divine, not in the hard, removed and objective controversies found in more patriarchal types of theology. Feminist theologies have engaged with postcolonial discourse, poststructuralists, queer theorists and many more in our quest to understand the experiences of women. We have tested our most cherished beliefs next to them and have emerged, after the debates, all the richer. For us the controversies are the life-blood, they signal that more unfolding is to be done and as each layer is peeled back more delights, more glorious revealing of the reality of women will be shown – the joys and the sorrows, the exaltation and the agony – but in this is the struggle – the continued struggle of feminist theologies to give voice to a more just and open world.

There are many issues we do not cover in depth here but remain implicit in the unfolding of feminist theologies. One such question that is touched in passing in the Christology chapter was posed a long time ago by Daphne Hampson[2] concerning the tension between autonomy, so central to feminist thinking, and the 'power over' that so much traditional theology seems to espouse. She asked, and we need to keep asking, who benefits when we give up freedoms and rights in our own lives. We know that this is not a straightforward question and the answer does not simply fall on the side of our rights and our freedoms. Mary Grey[3] has highlighted how it may be to the advantage of the globe if westerners gave up some of the rights they

---

2 Daphne Hampson, *Swallowing a Fishbone*, London: SPCK, 1996.

3 Mary Grey, *Sacred Longings: Ecofeminist Theology and Globalisation*, London: SCM Press, 2003.

think they have. Indeed, if we would reduce the comfort zone in our lives to the point where we may even feel that we are sacrificing some of our comforts, suffering perhaps, in order that the rest of the people on the planet may have enough and that the planet itself may breathe more easily. The lines are no longer clearly drawn with feminists on the side of back-to-nature and harmonious living, if we ever did actually think this was possible and indeed suggest it, versus those who are into the creation of capital through business enterprise. The picture is much more nuanced than that and in the secular world our feminist sisters are indeed suggesting that business and feminism do go together while we in theology continue to ask, on which backs and at what price? The controversies continue to emerge.

One area that is interesting and deserves attention is that of sexual rights for western women and the emergence of the so-called 'ladette' culture. Those of us who have fought so long and so hard for the rights of women to express themselves freely when it comes to sex are not sure what we make of some of the results. The commodification of sex by both male and female is not what we had in mind and the resultant 200,000 abortions a year in the United Kingdom is not defensible even by those of us who continue with all our hearts to defend a woman's right to choose. Of course patriarchy does still appear to be alive and well in these discourses on sex but we have to take note of what our efforts have given space for and perhaps we have to think cautiously through the issues. Our sisters from the East also draw our attention to the trade in foreign brides and the sex trade in general and ask if this is the price of women's assertiveness in the West. Is this really why western men are buying brides and using women from around the globe for sexual gratification? The new man is slow to emerge in the face of western feminist pressure; instead the old man has run to hide in the continued oppression of women. How are we to think ourselves through this question? We are not suggesting that we should give up the gains that western women have achieved, but perhaps we need to look at what may be the cost and to consider how to proceed in a more justice-seeking way. Castration not being an option!

On a more ethereal plane we have to face the fact that there are many controversies over whether we pray and if so to whom and with what expected result. No small matter. There is an explosion of women's liturgy books but they tell us very little, if anything, about the expected or at least hoped for outcome with the divine through these activities. Many theologians of course do not see a point in liturgical action beyond that of social cohesion and some form of self-affirmation on the part of the participants. Others are deeply troubled that feminist theologians have, as they see it, given ground on this matter and left it in the hands of patriarchal theology. Elizabeth Stuart is one such theologian who regrets what she sees as a forfeiting of the mystical dimension in feminist theologies. She applauds theologians who understand that there is much magic to make in the world and who continue to do so in their own way and for their own purposes quite apart from patriarchy. She says ' a belief in magic, in mysterious unseen forces, that can be summoned up and directed, empowers; it allows for the possibility that apparently small gestures or ritual actions can, in fact, change the world'.[4] These changes allow us to continue the work of redeeming or recreating the world, we create the space in which to think differently and to bring into play forces beyond what is visible. This view is indeed shared by some theologians, but for others the warning bells begin to peal along with the sanctuary bell. Stuart does not suggest that this mystical intervention should take the place of social action, but there is a fear that some will see it that way. Further, despite her claims that such a view allows for duality and not dualism, disconnection but not alienation,[5] there are many who fear that the battle which has been long-fought to move us away from the divided reality that places women on the back foot could be easily lost with the assertion of this theology. The controversy continues, and goes beyond the western patterns of feminist theologies.

---

4 Elizabeth Stuart, 'Exploding Mystery: Feminist Theology and the Sacramental' in *Feminist Theology*, Vol. 12:2 (2004), p. 230.

5 Stuart, 'Exploding Mystery', p. 231.

Beyond the West: Do developing world theologies speak with one voice?

Many times the controversies surrounding feminist theologies have been thought to be concentrated around a dichotomy between first and third-world women, That is to say that class and racial paradigms, or different approaches to gender and culture, were at the base of theological differences. It is true that early disputes among feminist theologians on the indifference or absence of perspectives from racism or classism, to give two examples, gave origin to a self-critical movement. This, as we will explore later, has also been exaggerated as there have been women theologians such as Rosemary Radford Ruether who engaged early on in a comprehensible feminist theological model which included a praxis from different models of women's oppression. Nevertheless, it was from those critical voices that wider reflections grew. From them, different emphases and methodologies have arisen. As an example, one could mention the fact that womanist methodology has been influential for the development of all feminist theologies worldwide, as remembrance and affirmation as part of a theological praxis based in liturgical and practical elements became the basic tenets of present-day feminist theologies. As women started to develop their theological praxis, some of the earliest casualties were essentialism and universal assumptions. In early discourses, there were voices and experiences which were absent. Leaving aside the fact that from women differences of all types of feminist theologies have been enriched, it is not correct to consider that first or developing world theologies function as a homogenous corpus. Yet, it has been difficult to expose or explore at times the controversies among non-western women theologians.

In fact, to assume that the main controversies in feminist theology were to be located between the two poles of western and developing world feminist theologians may need to be seen as part of the colonial legacy of theology in general. Specifically, the assumption has been that developing world feminist theologies didn't have internal controversies, nor among themselves (as for instance Latin American feminist theology), nor in their wider developing world context (Latin American feminist theologians and womanists, for instance, or mujeristas and Latinas). As we will see in this book, that has been a false assumption. Third-world feminist theologians have their differences too and are used to controversies. These are of an ideological nature or simply contextual. The developing world political and economic contexts produce theological priorities which require solidarity but also independent thinking. It is also a fact that our continents are more diverse in terms of culture and Christian traditions than has been acknowledged. In that sense, for instance, with all their commonalities, Central American theologians have characteristics that may differ in terms of analysis and interests from their South American counterparts, although this does not need to be an absolute norm. There are generational differences too: while a first generation of developing world women struggled for their right to be admitted to universities and seminaries and fought for ordination while pioneering the very first academic positions in the theological world, a much younger one finds different priorities on their agenda. The situation still may be hard in many countries in terms of ordination and theological education, but the mere existence of feminist theologies, networks of support and scholarships have produced substantial changes.

Among developing world feminist theologians, there are also strong disagreements concerning the role of the Virgin Mary and the conceptualization of gender and sexual identity. In these, we need to understand the fact that women constantly make choices, thematically and methodologically, which are pertinent to their contexts and communities and sometimes, the urgency of their situations. Moreover, this has become increasingly a factor for internal differences as more developing world women find academic and church positions abroad, and face challenges in their praxis-orientated theologies which are imposed by the constraints of western academia. The whole reflection on the meaning and praxis of the academic feminist theologian is relatively recent and bows to these new challenges.

It may be argued that the geographical diaspora of women theologians is another factor which adds to the rich diversity of feminist theologies. In the same way that developing world women may find themselves working in the western academy or church context, facing a different constituency of women, first-world women theologians are much more used to collaborating with projects, or to taking academic or ministerial positions in Latin America, Africa or Asia. In many cases the clear-cut theological identity of women, based on purely geographical criteria in the past, has been superceded by other criteria based on political options which include a postcolonial criticism of the theologians' own cultural and theological traditions too. In a way, developing world theologies do show today a spectrum of differences as wide as in the West, as liberation feminist theologies have succeeded in encouraging and celebrating the suppressed voices of women from the underside of history to develop their own theological positions. What at times seems to be a lack of unity, may only reflect the strength of the integrity of a theological movement that refuses to submit to stereotypes, or to respond theologically to agendas from the past. However, in this movement a further shift has occurred. That is, the feminist kernel in itself of 'feminist theologies' has changed.

Are all feminist theologians feminists?

The definition of patriarchy may be subjected today to more controversies than ever expected, bequeathed by the early 1970s when developing world feminist theologians wondered if their loyalty should be primarily with women or with marginalized communities of women and men. Many feminist theologians today view their analysis around structures grounded in particular constructions of masculinity which affect understandings of the relationship of economic, environmental and epistemological factors which also oppress men. The difference here is important and more nuanced than before, because it implies that although a theologian as for

instance, Robert Goss is not to be found under the label of
'feminist', he has more in common with developing world women
theologians working on sexuality than some other feminist theologians. For Goss, as Thomas Hanks or André Musskopft from Brazil,
share a liberationist kernel constructed around issues of social and
sexual justice which destabilizes the line between women and men
doing a gender/sexual-issued theology.

From here, we could be able to pinpoint another more recent controversy. One could argue that the sexual theologians are no longer
to be considered under the banner of feminism but perhaps some
form of postfeminists. In fact it is known in theological circles that
there are women theologians who use the term 'feminist' only for
strategical reasons, mainly to show solidarity with the historical
feminist struggle in church and society and to stand against the
recent backlash of antifeminist theological voices. By calling themselves postfeminist, they don't mean that they believe that feminism
is passé or irrelevant. In fact, the contrary must be true, but as the
'post' in 'postcolonial', postfeminism in theology reflects on the
fractured identity of women's struggles in the twenty-first century.
Postfeminist theologians may disagree with their feminist counterparts on issues such as pornography, pay less attention to gender
than to sexual constructions and work in the so-called 'hard-core
theology' under the umbrella of queer theologies. In reality, it means
that feminist camps are becoming wider than ever and there is a
community of women and men who, distancing themselves from
patriarcally based identities, become ideological allies in search of a
transformation of structures of patriarchal oppression at religious
and societal levels.

At the end of the twentieth century, differences among feminist
theologians were far more than geographical or cultural controversies. The definition of feminism has become divisive too, but it has
always been. That, in itself has been a positive achievement, because
the mere term 'feminism' or 'feminist' has forced us to cross certain
neutral territory and to declare a reflection and an action, that is, a
definitive theological praxis from a woman's locus. It may be still the

case in many countries where to declare themselves feminist put academic and church women in a target position. However, many developing world women theologians were among the first feminists who sensed the need to introduce a postcolonial perspective in their definition of feminism. That has given space to a theological emphasis on women's identity from their own cultural and religious non-Christian discourses. They also introduced at an early stage the genre of testimony in feminist theologies, in an effort to reflect the class, racial and gender rupture that developing world feminist theologies represent. Thematically, this gave place to a rich space were motherhood has been revalued in different categories from western feminism. In this, for instance, we may remember the category of mothering from the womanist and the political mother of Latin American theologians. In feminism, women's bodies became texts, and in feminist theologies, there are different approaches to the text of women's bodies. Specifically, developing world theologians have in common with western sisters their political project to transform conceptual structures of power which oppresses people and the planet alike.

This book deals with some of the key areas of systematic theology where different responses have been given to this challenge to produce a different Christian vision which could become a faith in action, and an action of transformation. It offers an understanding of how the diverse feminist theologies approach the challenges of our century. This is of course not a definitive work as feminist theologies do not really go in for that, it is rather a contribution to the ongoing debate. It also asks that crucial question that has been raised by some as to whether there is an ongoing debate to be had, is there indeed a future for feminist theologies? Have they, through their diversity, failed to make an impact and made themselves internally unfit for the task of transformation? With so many voices emerging has any hope of a unified agenda disappeared for ever? Unified agendas fulfil an important role in the struggle for social and sexual rights. Yet, they also tend to restrict them. Women tend to disappear easily under the label of 'theologies from the poor' or 'developing world theology'.

Political theologies, by definition, have never considered the reflection and experience of women, nor the diverse agenda of change that
feminist theologies demand.

This book

This book is not an introduction to feminist theologies. There are
several books already dedicated to that theme. This book's goal is
to provide the reader with a sense of the diversity and conflict that
surrounds a living contextual theological reflection such as the
feminist theological one. For that, we have made a selection of some
of the most important current themes and discussions in the field.
Some, such as the christological debates, are well documented.
Other discussions, such as those of feminist liberation theologies
and sexuality, are more recent and still hotly debated in the corridors of conferences and gatherings. In that sense, we have also
reflected the debates that we have heard in recent years during the
annual gatherings of the British and Irish Feminist School of
Theology. As an example of this point, we can mention the discussions we had among theologians and feminist Christian women on
issues of using a more accessible theological language.

The other thing this book is not meant to provide is a guide to
each of the many women theologians worldwide concerning these
current debates. For reasons of space and in order to make this book
more user-friendly, we have concentrated mainly on a group of
theologians from the North Atlantic scene, but this does not imply
that other very important theological voices do not have a position
on the issues discussed here.

Basically, one of our objectives has been, precisely, to give a sense
of the aliveness and freshness of feminist theologies by showing how
controversies and disagreements always have had an important role
to play. Moreover, without these controversial debates and at times,
almost opposite theological positions, the feminist theological
movement could not have reached the grade of maturity, originality

and transgression which characterizes its reflection and its action. At the end of the day, feminist theologies are theologies concerned with social transformation, and that includes the need to take different theological positions in regards to methods, themes but also strategies concerning issues such as the ordination of women and debates on sexuality, which tend to be influential in the implementation of laws concerning abortion, contraception and marriage and divorce issues in many countries.

We have divided this book into six chapters, each dealing with a particular aspect of method or dogmatic reflection where controversies are most frequent. Chapter 1 deals with the fundamental question of gender and sexuality and the ever-shifting ground both these areas have become. It is a fundamental question because after all if we do not have women we do not have an experiential base from which to create feminist theology. However this has become hotly disputed, What is a woman? and How may we speak of any experiential base in an authentic manner? are not the simple questions they may once have seemed. With the increasing work in the area of gender and the now accepted notion that gender is a performance, we are asked to think again about the way in which we understand the foundational identity of woman. The other huge area feminist theologies have addressed is that of sexuality which is in itself being affected by the shifting ground of the gender debate. Both these areas, which may at first glance appear to have little impact on traditional theology, actually shake it to the core since so much traditional theology, which has always claimed it is above and beyond and thus unaffected by human enfleshment, is developed on the back of embedded notions of sex and gender.

Chapter 2, 'Myths Surrounding Feminist Theological Hermeneutics' deals with the key questions surrounding feminist theological methods. Although it is true that we have commonalities in the sense of basing our analysis around women's experiences and mediator sciences such as gender studies, in addition to sociopolitical and cultural methods, it is also true that those methods are not neutral. The more recent controversies about queer theology and sexuality illustrate the point. Not every feminist theologian uses queer theory as part of their critical analysis. In the same way, conceptualizations of race vary among Latin Americans and Black American women.

Chapter 3, 'The Virgin Mary: Many Images, Many Interests' explores some of the controversies surrounding feminist mariological approaches. These are not just geographically located as in, for instance, the reflections on Mary from Asia or Latin America and Europe or the United States, but recently have shown new fractures in the discourse. That is to say that if in the beginning feminist theologians were preoccupied with Mariology in a similar way as to Christology, focusing on issues of women's identity and agency, the debates have now taken a different turn by considering how particular patriarchal sexual epistemologies have contributed to the formation of mariological discourses. Therefore, the so-called 'Mariologies of liberation' have been further interrogated. However, the theologies which advocate a disruption of Mariologies as inherently oppressive have also received challenges, for instance, from postcolonial studies. Women have not been passive bearers of patriarchal theologies but have managed to produce their own counter-discourses. Mariology is, in many instances, one example of these subversive theological women's practices which may have contributed not only to women's survival in Christianity but also to their own empowering.

Chapter 4 deals with Christology which right from the beginning has been an area of passionate debate. Can a male saviour save women? was no idealist question, it struck at the heart of a patriachally constructed Christ and opened the flood gates to further and more refined questions – Can he save black women, lesbians, Asian women, white disabled women, the socially and economically disadvantaged? the list is endless. What has emerged from these debates has been a much expanded christological debate. Furthermore the dualistic underpinning of the traditional Christ has been dislodged and the incarnate one has begun to emerge with devastating economic and social questions around that shared reality. The question we are being forced to face in this new century is how far we can push the paradigm before it finally crumbles and if it crumbles do we burst forth into our full incarnate potential or do we lose something along the way. These are exciting times for those who have the courage.

Chapter 5 deals with life after death – a topic at the centre of much debate in feminist theologies. Many feminist theologians who have pointed out the harmful effects of dualistic thinking wish us to give up on this final frontier of non-reality, a world in which to place our anxieties and avoid the real questions. They also claim that this promise of a world beyond continues to avert attention from the ecological crisis facing us. They may be right, but there are others who argue that if we do not have a space beyond in which we may think differently then all we do is repeat the same mistakes in the now. It is interesting to see how those who would have very much the same political agenda are poles apart in relation to this question. The real tension appears to lie between those who would not give up on the utopian thinking, but would wish to give up on the utopian place called heaven; if incarnation is to be truly powerful it may be argued that it has to be an ever-unfolding reality in the here and now and not have some other dimension. My own feeling is that the more we explore quantum thought, the nearer we will get to understanding this tension.

Chapter 6, 'Controversies on the Future of Feminist Theology' intends to be, more than a final conclusion, a continuation of the controversial debates in feminist theologies by reflecting on how the future is being perceived. There have been many books, articles and conferences in the past decade dedicated to the issue of the future of all contextual theologies, including feminist ones. The discussions have been happening on different fronts. For instance, the use of the scriptures, the extent of the canonical corpus, the theoretical framework of analysis chosen and yes, the viability or not of feminist theologies at the time of postmodern discourses and globalization processes which, gender wise, are less discriminatory in terms of exploitation and oppression. Also, as said before, queer theologies have changed the gender balance of feminist theologies as, for instance, many queer men work closely with queer women. Meanwhile different alliances are produced and the struggle for equality becomes a struggle for the right to be different. Yet, in the midst of all, women's religious oppression seems to have reached new peaks, not just in the Christian churches where still the debates about women's ordination and theological education go on, but as reflected in the influence of Christian leaders in the secular legislation of many countries.

In the end, feminist theologies do not need a homogenous agenda or a hierarchically led set of priorities. In fact, feminist theologies have shown their growing maturity by moving away from these orders. It may even be that feminist theologies are moving away from systematic theology. In fact, statistics may show that women are not so keen to do research on what is thought by many to be the last bastion of patriarchal theologies: the systematic theological field at least, not without introducing some innovative and at times controversial perspectives. Some of us consider that the call is to disrupt the structures of sin which lie at the centre of the traditional way of doing theology and the thematical organization of the key themes for theological reflection. The call may be, precisely, the contrary: to continue producing an increasingly a-systematic theology which may allow new questions and different sorts of interrogations to take place among different theological subjects who are women, straight or queer, from the North Atlantic or developing world margins of theological power.

It is our hope that this book will help to highlight some of the current debates and controversies in feminist theologies, but also, to stimulate new ones. As feminist or post-feminist theologians, we constitute one of the largest disruptive theological groups that the twenty-first century has produced. We have changed the way that theology is thought, spoken and even methodologically conceived. In fact, if the Holy Spirit moves in history, it has moved largely among dispossessed, oppressed women from different continents. We pray that the process will continue and, therefore, the continuous struggle to unmask patriarchal ideological discourses on

God and Christianity. At the end of the day, feminist theologians have argued and disagreed with each other on many issues because this is a kind of discourse where honesty is required. The kind of theological honesty required to liberate not only women but also God from the distorting effects of patriarchal power. In that sense, feminist theologies truly represent the liberation of theology movement.

1

Gender and Sexuality

It may seem redundant to say so but in order for there to be feminist theologies there have to be women! That is to say there needs to be an identifiable group whose experience can be used as the starting point for the reflection and theological revolution. In addition, of course, the group has to be distinct enough from other groups to warrant particular attention. In the early days of the women's movement and of feminist theology, it was never in doubt that women formed a distinct category which generated questions and issues appropriate to them. However, theory moves on and we find that even the reality of 'woman' is being called into question as we shall see as the chapter progresses. We are in exciting times in the area of feminist scholarship, because if the very concept of woman is being questioned, then have we become outdated and no longer needed as feminist theologians? Even a quick glance around our global community will show us that the disparity between male and female continues to exist from pay deferentials and glass ceilings to torture, death, and lack of rights across a wide range of areas in everyday life. Such a picture makes the continuation of feminist theology imperative for as long as it remains true that being in a female body carries with it unequal treatment and oppression then those who will continue to question the justice of such ways of being are needed. In our view then the move to understanding human persons as having more 'blended identities' is engaging and exciting at the theoretical level but needs to be placed alongside the lived reality of women in different cultural, racial, economic and social situations – not all our sisters have the luxury of living at a theoretical level. The question that feminist theology is constantly battling with is whether the theory changes the practice or the praxis the theory – as we struggle we need to be ever mindful of the gendered bodies of women and female children as they bear the weight of the systems.

Christianity has historically been blind to questions of gender believing that 'mankind' includes the experiences of women and men and encompasses all that makes us human. This assumption of course works in many ways, to a certain extent it becomes self-fulfilling in that women do begin to understand themselves through the male lens and in so many respects begin to see themselves as defective, insufficient or as simply experientially deluded. As de Beauvoir realized, all those years ago, a woman is not born she is made, and her making is in order to support the male-dominated status quo, she is made into what is useful. And as she also so movingly noted women apprehend their own bodies not as 'instruments of her transcendence but as an object destined for another'.[1] This destination is usually the physical male but can also be the great Phallus in the sky, the patriarchal father who invades all manner of relationships. Once invaded the 'intimate recesses of the personality . . . it may maim and cripple the spirit for ever'.[2]

Although God plays no part in our secular society, it has to be acknowledged that this making of women has its roots in theology since the way in which men and women are meant to be supposedly reflects God's design for the universe. For example, the inequality between the sexes has been and still is attributed to the notion of complementarity which can be derived from a patriarchal reading of the Genesis myth. Eve is taken from the side of Adam, thereby signalling that the two halves need to be made whole once more. Woman being a derivative of man can never expect to possess the original, holy qualities to the same extent. This is not just a view that can be lifted from the Hebrew scriptures, some scholars also argue it

---

1 Quoted in Sandra Lee Bartky, *Femininity and Domination*, New York: Routledge, 1990, p. 38.

2 Bartky, *Femininity and Domination*, p. 58.

is there in what at first seems a very positive statement for women, the Pauline injunction regarding equality in Christ (Gal. 3.28). On closer inspection it is argued that what is actually assumed is that woman disappears, the rib slots neatly back into place and the male image of God is left as he was first placed on this earth. In Christ the breach that occurred in Genesis is healed and man once again shines in unitary glory.[3] Presumably it is not beyond the bounds of speculation to assume that at the eschaton woman will cease to exist, but until that time she will be judged against an androcentric norm. Borresen argues that Christ had to be incarnate as a male if he was to represent perfect humanity, such is the weight of patriarchal ideology.[4] It would have been inconceivable to the Fathers that a woman might be the divine incarnate. Indeed, for them it was often hard to imagine that woman could be holy. This is a trend which started in Ephesians where we are told that woman's salvational equality is gained by achieving Christlike maleness (Eph. 4.13). It was picked up and carried on with vigour, Tertullian imagining that resurrected women would be a mixture of angels and men, while Jerome thought that if a woman wished to serve Christ she had to give up being a woman (*Exposition of the Gospel of Luke*, 10.161), while Ambrose added that a believing woman does indeed progress to complete manhood (*Regula Episcopi*, Preface). This gender-bending for salvation is evident in much Christian history and paints an interesting and nuanced picture of the place of gender in the Christian narrative.

The story of Thecla presents us with an interesting character in this respect who may show another world of gender-understanding. Is she a transvestite or is her story used as a motif to tell us something of significance about the relationship of people who become Christian with their gendered environment? Contemporary scholarship is no longer content simply to accept the argument that she and others cross-dressed for the sake of safety when they were on

---

3 Kari Borresen, *The Image of God*, Minneapolis: Fortress Press, 1995, p. 62.
4 Borresen, *The Image of God*, p. 190

missionary journeys. After all in Thecla's story she does not cross-dress from the beginning, even though she is travelling and at some risk, she only cross-dresses after baptism. And of course, this is in strict contravention of scriptural command (Deut. 22.5). Transvestites were not unknown in this world as they were quite common in some pagan cults where they were associated with Aphrodite of Cyprus, however this does not help explain the newly baptized Thecla taking on male dress. The clue to Thecla may be found when she is thrown to the beasts but not killed, the tale relays that she found herself clothed by God. John Anson suggests that this is perhaps a literal fulfilment of the putting on of Christ that Paul speaks about in baptism and so for him the donning of men's clothes is simply another step in this process that started in the arena with the beasts.[5] He continues that a faith based in Galatians 3.27-28 would mean followers would embody a state of primal perfection that overcame all distinctions including that of sex. In putting on Christ, followers would attempt to appropriate his male form.[6] But is the only option to her to see perfect creation as male and so to drag it up in order to be saved! Was that really how the women themselves understood their actions or is this simply more wishful thinking on behalf of the male hierarchy of the time and the male interpreters since? The Gospel of Thomas may certainly be seen as the drag king's gospel where it reads, 'For every woman who has become male will enter the kingdom of heaven.'[7] Of course this was made quite explicit in some baptismal rites such as those among the Valentinians, where bisexual fusion was enacted and women were transformed into males.

---

5 John Anson, 'The Female Transvestite in Early Monasticism: The Origin and Development of a Motif', *Viator*, Vol. 5 (1974), pp. 1-32.

6 Anson, 'The Female Transvestite', p. 7.

7 Jean Doresse, *The Secret Books of the Egyptian Gnostics: An Introduction to the Gnostic Coptic Manuscripts Discovered at Chenoboskion with an English translation and Critical Evaluation of the Gospel of Thomas*, New York: Harper, 1960, p. 370.

Another possible background for Thecla's actions may have been rooted in Montanism where the women prophets Prisca and Maximilla had prominent roles. They had visions which led them to understand themselves as female Christs, an understanding which was based in their reading of Galatians 3.27–28, a text which suggested to them that once the distinctions and divisions of class, race and gender were overcome they were free to embrace their divine natures. It seems perfectly possible to argue that they understood their male attire as a signal of overcoming the binary opposites of gender that set in place unequal lived reality. In taking seriously the message of equality of the Christian gospel, they queered gender-performance in order to find a way of living the radical equality they professed to believe. After all once we engage in confusing the categories it leads to their breakdown as oppositional points of reference. It seems entirely possible that these stories of gender-bending were written by and for women who wished to subvert the social order. Possibly they represented wishes rather than realities at the time that they were written, but it may also be the case that they traced back to the time of Jesus and had a kernel of truth embedded in the lives of women around him. Women who break out from the norm in any age face the threat of physical violence and I find it extremely fascinating that their way of remaining safe was to keep transgressing the norm.[8] Women like Thecla both cut their hair and wear male clothing which is an extremely transgressive action in the world in which she is portrayed. These women were not all transsexual but they did push the gender boundaries very hard in order to create space in which to flourish. Their stories need to be understood in a very different light than that cast by the Fathers who celebrate the putting aside of female natures in order to become holy men of God. These women were, we believe, doing something more

---

8 See Lisa Isherwood (ed.), *The Good News of the Body: Sexual Theology and Feminism*, Sheffield: Sheffield Academic Press, 2000. In the conclusion I argue that safe sex for women in this day and age is transgressive sex since playing the game has got us nowhere. It seems our sisters in faith had the same idea.

profound: they were challenging the restricting and deadening gender-performances that did not allow for the flourishing of full humanity. As Judith Butler[9] has since noted, the performance of gender places a deep and deathlike sadness in our psyches as it cuts us off from at least half of what we might be. Our foresisters in faith appear to be asking questions about engendered spaces that are as relevant today as they were then, and they show that storytelling and action can be subversive.

We see just how embedded questions of gender are in western culture when we look to the 'fathers' of another kind, those of philosophy and psychology – they like the Church Fathers before them place women on the back foot. Gender is inscribed on the body and the bodies of women have carried a very heavy burden under patriarchy. The way in which the bodies of women and men have been ascribed gender roles is a question of power and significance in the world, and these definitions do not simply show the difference they *make* the difference, and as such need much attention by feminist theologies. The way in which the bodies of women and the gender roles given them have been viewed by the churches and traditional theology has meant that women are denied access to the symbolic order in any creative and positive way. They are the abject, the ones that have to be rejected in order that the symbolic and political realm can work.

Both Foucault and Lacan have taken up the issues of power and knowledge and the entry into the symbolic order through the acquisition of language. For Foucault discourse is much more than language as it is embedded in material form in both cultural and social institutions. Therefore subjectivity is found within the material practices of everyday life. This is not an open-ended engagement since he also proposes that modernity saw the triumph of medicalization and so our bodies have become victims to the normalizing power of an external discourse. In addition he claims

---

9 Judith Butler, *The Psychic Life of Power*, California: Stanford University Press, 1997.

we are in a crisis brought on by the waning power of metaphysics and the decline of the Enlightenment which have both led to the reassessing of reason as the motor of historical progress. If reason alone is not central, then it seems acceptable that the body should be at the centre of discourse, but at the same time it is the victim of discourse. The multiplicity of discourses claiming both knowledge and normativity for their view of the body has meant, 'the body emerges at the centre of theoretical and political debate at exactly the time of history when there is no more consensus about what the body actually is'.[10] The paradox then is that at the same time as opening up discussions about the body, the body itself has been closed down by learned discourses about shape, size, function and form all of which are speaking to it and not hearing it. Foucault's body is created by power, but of course it can also resist through acts of deviance and perversion because the self in the body is not an essence but rather a strategic possibility. With power comes resistance and indeed a multiplicity of resistances which when made strategic can cause a revolution.[11] For Foucault this was embodied and he advocates seeking new pleasures which liberate our desires from the male genital discourse, for him fist-fucking, S&M and fetishism could be viewed as ways to dislocate this discourse as they all place desire and satisfaction in other and unexpected parts of the body. There is then a genuine body relocation and with it the chance of a new discourse.

Lacan as we all know may well be called the father of the Phallus! For him the Symbolic Order is what defines us as embodied persons and following Freud he makes it very difficult for women to find a place at all in this order of the fathers. For him the acquisition of language is extremely important and even this is different for boys and girls since girls do not speak the language of the father which is

10 Kathleen Lennon and Margaret Whitford, *Knowing the Difference: Feminist Perspectives in Epistemology*, London: Routledge, 1994, p. 19.

11 David. M. Halperin, *Saint Foucault: Towards a Gay Hagiography*, Oxford: Oxford University Press, 1995, p. 125.

the dominant currency. Sexual/gender difference then is at the centre of the Symbolic Order and the Phallus reigns supreme as the structuring principle; this of course is developed from a very uncritical acceptance of the Freudian notion of the Oedipus complex. It creates a world in which women and our bodies are always lacking, indeed Lacan speaks of women as absences which need to be filled with phallic signifiers. There is no way to resolve this situation within the world of the Symbolic Order and Lacan urges women to find their own economy beyond that of the phallus. This can be done through female sexual pleasure (jouissance) but it is never likely to be achieved since it is beyond the phallic and therefore beyond language and meaning itself. There can be no subjectivity then and women and their bodies can only find significance through the male body and the male symbolic. This situation permeates the whole of culture where women are constantly on the outside without a language to call their own. Our bodies then have no hope of a voice in the discourses that are played out on them. Irigaray highlights this dilemma by suggesting that there can be no subjectivity until women find a place in culture since this belonging gives psychic leverage to our personhood.[12] For Irigaray this can begin with the body, we can find a language when our genital lips meet and speak. She also feels that we have to find a language of the divine; in fact the two processes are not that distinct. It is a matter of great urgency that we find a language because if we do not then we simply repeat the same history through an inability to think otherwise. Irigaray's contribution to religious philosophy is well known to readers and what is perhaps of most relevance here is her insistence that women have to find a place in culture, a tradition, in order to empower them. It has been argued by some that sociologists of the body have often forgotten the materiality and social contexts of bodies in their prioritization of Lacan and the psychoanalytic discourse, the one that gets us in the most intimate parts of ourselves, our psyches.

---

12 Alexandra Howson, *Embodying Gender*, London: Sage, 2005, p. 103.

Both Butler and Braidotti challenge the Lacanian notion that women are outside language, Butler through suggesting that woman is in process and so not a finally defined other who can be placed outside. She is a body becoming, this is a language of its own, a language of materiality.[13] Braidotti, meanwhile, speaks of figurations which are politically informed accounts of alternative subjectivity. This living 'as if' is 'a technique of strategic re-location in order to rescue what we need of the past in order to trace paths of trans-formations of our lives here and now'. She continues, '"as if" is affirmation of fluid boundaries, practice of the intervals' which sees nothing as an end in itself[14] – not even the Symbolic Order one suspects! While she does acknowledge that we as women have no mother tongue, we do have linguistic sites from which we both see and fail to see. For this reason then we need to be nomads, taking no position or identity as permanent but rather trespassing and trans-gressing, making coalitions and interconnections beyond boxes. No language but we do have bodies, bodies that have been 'the basic stratum on which the multilayered institution of Phallocentric subjectivity is erected [they are] the primary matter and the foundational stone, whose silent presence installs the master in his monologic mode'.[15] These same bodies can be radically subverting of culture when they find their voice beyond the fixed language and meaning of the master's discourses. Braidotti anticipates the objection that total nomadism will never allow for coalitions by sug-gesting that the only way to find a larger vision is to be somewhere in particular, to engage in a politics of positioning.[16] However, this does not require us to be static or defined by male definitions, because as she tells us, it is the feminine that is a 'typically masculine

---

13 Judith Butler, *Gender Trouble: Feminism and the Subversion of Gender*, London: Routledge, 1990, p. 30.

14 Rosi Braidotti, *Nomadic Subjects: Embodiment and Sexual Difference in Contemporary Feminist Theory*, New York: Columbia University Press, 1994, p. 6.

15 Braidotti, *Nomadic Subjects*, p. 119.

16 Braidotti, *Nomadic Subjects*, p. 73.

attitude which turns male disorders into feminine values',[17] and not the female body; this is free to roam and to express itself. To find new ways of being by thinking through the body.

Christian history shows us the extent to which power has been exerted over bodies in the name of divine truth and the crippling results of definite and unchanging gender stereotypes. Feminism, by emphasizing the centrality of women's experience, has given power to challenge that to date has never been known. The women's movement claimed that women had the right, based on their own experience, to define their own lives. This is a revolution under patriarchal Christianity which claims the right of definition for itself and the male God. Slowly women are coming to understand what it means to be human in a way no longer defined by the dominant culture. To no longer be the 'other'. Irigaray, challenges de Beauvoir's definition of woman as the Other, seeing even this 'Otherness' as constructed by patriarchy. Therefore, to begin a critique of the dominant culture from the place of otherness is nonetheless to place oneself within that culture. Women therefore need to find a way to be 'where they are' undefined and free. It can be argued that both the history and the destiny of women are written on their bodies through the inscription of gender. In addition though the female body can offer a new paradigm, a new knowledge, one that challenges the traditional word. With the adoption of feminist methodology in theology we have a revolutionary situation in which embodied subjectivity is placed at the heart of knowing and this declares invalid 'objective absolute rationality' which has been the 'norm' within patriarchal mythology.

Feminists who have been creating theology have from the beginning understood that God is not a concept that can be treated separately or with different tools from the rest of the created order. Indeed, it is the conception of God that creates the world the way it is including the allocation of gender and sex. So we were never naïve enough to think that gender would be transformed through the

---

17 Braidotti, *Nomadic Subjects*, p. 124.

worship of the great phallic God, we always knew we would have to challenge that God and that the place to start would be in regaining confidence in our own subjectivity. This was not an easy matter as we had to find a basis for it, and in starting with the body we were also faced with all the layers of patriarchal readings of that body and so have found 'body theology' to be a difficult and at times painful process of unmasking and laying bare.

Although we knew about subjectivity we were not always so good at getting to grips with it, and so all those years ago when feminist theology was in its infancy, the whole question of gender was a simple one – there were women and men and the latter had done the former wrong! All that was needed was for women to unite around central questions and the whole gender question could be sorted out and justice would reign. Now that we are a little wiser it appears that we were too quick to accept the master's definitions of the 'woman' question. In asserting a female identity, which of course seems to be necessary for a feminist theology to follow on, perhaps we were not critical enough in considering what that might mean. Certainly from the start our black sisters reminded us that all female experience is not the same and for that reason they adopted the 'womanist' title. Clearly the female took various forms according to context and economic, political, cultural and regional location. She was many things. Audre Lorde[18] called Mary Daly to account in the very early days for appearing to speak with one woman's voice. Subjectivity opened up a whole world and perhaps we were not fully aware that subjectivity will never allow the comfort of the old unified certainties to re-emerge, not even those around who women are, what women want and how it is for women. We had not fully purged the master's ways, we perhaps looked for a unified world even if we called it 'global sisterhood'. What we had done was to actually shatter the unified convenience of 'woman' and open up a kaleidoscope of potential and a rainbow of glorious harmony and disharmony in the unfolding of the 'reality' of woman. Once we moved from concepts

---

18 Audre Lorde, *Sister Outsider*, California: Crossing Press, 1984.

like woman, female, feminine, there would be no end to what was laid before us through the lived reality of women's lives.

Critics of feminist theologies often cite this open space, this embrace of endless possibility as the weakness of the discipline. Surely we need to fix something in order to have a discipline related to anything at all – surely we need women to have feminist theology?! But has it not been the simple definitions that have led over the centuries to the exclusions? Butler[19] is once again provocative when she declares that multiplicity is not the thing that makes agency impossible but it is rather the very nature of agency, precisely the condition in which agency flourishes. Further she suggests that it is in the fear of the questions posed by multiplicity that we find the creation of the rhetoric of morals as a defence of politics.[20] She illustrates her point through considering how the Catholic Church deals with issues of gender and sexual difference. The Curia has called for the United Nations to eliminate the language of gender from its platforms to do with the status of women, declaring that the word is simply a cover for homosexuality which they condemn and do not see as having a place in a rights agenda. They insisted on a return to the word 'sex' and their rhetoric attempted to indisputably link sex with maternal and feminine, reflecting as they saw it the divinely ordained 'natural goodness' of things. To those observing, the agenda was very clear; it was an attempt to reverse many of the gains that women had made in relation to human rights, and it was a narrow defining that could be once again placed at the service of containment and control. Butler puts it as follows: 'the Vatican fears the separation of sexuality from sex, for that introduces a notion of sexual practice that is not constrained by putatively natural reproductive ends'.[21] It is then no surprise to her that the Vatican considers the inclusion of lesbian rights in United Nations legislation as 'anti-human'. Given their understanding of the relation of sex and the human person, it is

---

19 Judith Butler, *Undoing Gender*, London: Routledge, 2004.
20 Butler, *Undoing Gender*, p. 180.
21 Butler, *Undoing Gender*, p. 184.

correct to make such a statement since the inclusion of lesbian into the realm of the universal would be to expand the boundaries of what is so far defined as human within the conventional limits. In order that all humans may be recognized, it seems that 'the human must become strange to itself'.[22]

Butler goes on to say that this new human 'will have no ultimate form but it will be one that is constantly negotiating sexual difference in a way that has no natural or necessary consequences for the social organisation of sexuality'.[23] Is this what those early Christian fore-sisters were attempting to embody in their interpretation of the declaration in Galatians? Is it in this enactment of the beyond, the becoming strange to oneself, that all the possibilities of incarnate life find root? Butler reminds us that the body is the site on which language falters[24] and the signifiers of the body remain for the most part largely unconscious, which in itself is a language, but one ever-unfolding and of many tongues. Performativity is a whole body engagement just as incarnation is and both resist the deadening claws of narrow and controlling definitions of personhood – both expand the edges of where it is we think we inhabit.

For feminist theology gender is an important and far-reaching concept, as we would argue it always has been from the early days of the Jesus movement.[25] It is crucial that we push against the narrow definitions of sex that lend themselves to strict political as well as religious boundaries and borders, of the psyche, spiritual, economic and social. Although the idea of woman is becoming more complex, and some would argue is disappearing under the weight of the new theorizing, it is important that we too do not fall back into narrow and fear-filled definitions that do not allow the full becoming of the human/divine person.

The other massive contribution offered by feminist theologies is

---

22 Butler, *Undoing Gender*, p. 191.

23 Butler, *Undoing Gender*, p. 191.

24 Butler, *Undoing Gender*, p. 198.

25 See Lisa Isherwood, *The Power of Erotic Celibacy: Queering Hetero-patriarchy*, London: T&T Clark, 2006, Chapter 2.

in the area of sexuality. The traditional interpretation of Christianity has not looked kindly on sexuality – particularly the sexuality of women which lives in the Christian psyche as the cause of the Fall of Man! Many of the early feminist scholars illustrated for us how women, sexuality, spirituality and the sacred were not always at odds in our human history. Indeed, women's sexuality was for many centuries intimately and positively connected with the sacred and the divine itself.[26] This changed dramatically with the establishment of Christianity and scholars also documented this shift for us. However, we were not only made aware of what had been lost, but were given ways of reinstating what was lost, of once again placing female sexuality within the realm of the sacred. It is this recovery of the erotic within theology that has marked a significant contribution of feminist theologies.

For theologians, Audre Lorde, although not a theologian herself, stands out as the provider of the essential canon on the erotic. For Lorde the erotic is the intense kernel of our being that when released 'flows through and colours my life with a kind of energy that heightens and sensitizes and strengthens all my experience'.[27] It is a form of outreaching joy that connects us to all things and transforms all experiences into delight. This erotic joy is physical, intellectual, psychic and emotional and forms a solid bridge between people which continues to allow difference but lessens the threat that difference is often perceived to contain. It is a profound teacher as it allows the kind of closeness that produces our deepest knowledge which in turn leads to the transformation of the world. Lorde says, 'recognizing the power of the erotic within our lives can give us the energy to pursue genuine change within our world, rather than merely settling for a shift of characters in the same weary drama'.[28] It is deeply ethical in both its nature and the effect it strives to have.

Rita Brock and Carter Heyward are the two feminist theologians

---

26 See for example, Tess Tessier, *Dancing After the Whirlwind*, Boston: Beacon Press, 1997.

27 Lorde, 'Uses of the Erotic' in *Sister Outsider*, p. 57.

28 Lorde, *Sister Outsider*, p. 59.

who expand this understanding and are most associated with the notion of Christ as erotic power. Rita Brock believes that when speaking of Jesus as powerful we have to be quite clear that this is erotic power; this is no abstract concept but is power deeply embedded in our very core. This kind of power is wild and cannot be controlled, and living at this level saves us from the sterility that comes from living by the head alone. Eros allows us to feel our deepest passions in all areas of life and to reclaim it from the narrow sexual definition that has been used by patriarchal understanding. Christianity has always encouraged agapé which Brock sees as heady and objective and therefore not as something that will change the world. Indeed it is part of the objectifying discourse which allows us to stand by as though powerless in the face of many of the horrors of our world. Both Brock and Heyward show how in fearing passion, traditional Christianity has made us a passionless and therefore largely impotent people. They both argue that agapé may have a place but it is the embrace of Eros that will engage us, and so can change the world.

In Brock's words:

> Heart is our original grace. In exploring the depths of heart we find incarnate in ourselves the divine reality of connection, of love . . . But its strength lies in fragility. To be born so open to the presence of others in the world gives us the enormous, creative capacity to make life whole. Yet such openness means that the terrifying and destructive factors of life are also taken into the self, a self that then requires loving presence to be restored to grace.[29]

It is in finding our heart that we realize how we have been damaged and our original grace has become distorted. This memory and the anger we should feel at this memory opens us to our deepest passions and it is here that our erotic power lies. A power that is enhanced by relationship, not by control and dominance, erotic

---

29 Rita Brock, *Journeys by Heart: A Christology of Erotic Power*, New York: Crossroad, 1988, p. 17.

power is indeed wild as the Fathers counselled us but for this it is also beautiful and divine.

Heyward's starting point for seeking to understand God is taking human experience seriously. She says: 'We are, left alone untouched until, we choose to take ourselves – our humanity – more seriously than we have taken our God.'[30] For Heyward, intimacy is the deepest quality of relation and she sees no reason why it should be left out of our theological story. Heyward believes that to be intimate is to be assured that we are known in such a way that the mutuality of our relation is real, creative and cooperative and so it has a fundamental part in any theology and religious practice. She is highly provocative wondering as she does whether within a patriarchal world this kind of depth of relationality can be achieved between women and men, or whether it is a whole lot easier between women. I have often argued that it would be more than a pity if her huge challenge based on daring scholarship were sidelined by those who find it too difficult simply through the excuse of what appears to be a lesbian agenda. I do not believe that there is such an agenda but rather an honest questioning of just how it is for women who attempt mutuality with men when both have been subject to the divisive rhetoric of patriarchy. It is a question worth asking and I am not sure we are anywhere close to an answer – there are those among us who would like to think we are. Heyward's original work was rooted in a close analysis of Mark's Gospel and a rereading of the meaning of *exousia* and *dunamis* as used in that Gospel. Her conclusions led her to assert that it is the power of *dunamis*, that raw dynamic energy that attracts us to each other and the world, that is the transforming, and thus salvific, power that Jesus points us towards through his life and engagement with just such a passion. There is no need to dissect Heyward's arguments here[31] rather simply to acknowledge that her grounding of passion, and erotic power within the christological

---

30 Carter Heyward, *The Redemption of God*, Lanham: University of America Press, 1982, p. xix.

31 See as above or Lisa Isherwood, *Liberating Christ*, Cleveland, OH: Pilgrim Press, 1999, chapter 5.

arena opened the way for much creative and revolutionary sexual theology, and with it rethinking of women's sexuality in general. Christology and sexuality are intimately related in the theological method of Heyward and this creates a deep challenge that the churches will in the long run find hard to ignore. If the central core of Christian belief, Christology, is indeed rooted in the erotic, which has some expression through the sexual, then Christian theologians will have to think again about their naïve division of these deeply human, deeply divine elements of humanity.

Indeed, the whole way in which we are now able to speak of sexual theology is in large part due to writers such as Heyward who, using a feminist methodology, allowed experience to be the starting point rather than the declarations about actions and feelings that had been the traditional church starting point. This feminist engagement with female sexuality gave ways in which women could lift their bodies and sexuality out of the mire of male clerical dictate and once again declare the sacredness of their sexual lives. Of course, in turn, this also highlighted how, under patriarchal rules both clerical and secular, the lived reality of women's sexuality was not always as free or sacred – many a woman has had her body made the object of blasphemous treatment by clerical declaration as well as physically harsh and disrespectful treatment. We were able to look again and with new critical tools at issues such as domestic violence, rape and child abuse as well as looking very positively at a range of women's preferred sexual activities and choices. As with the women's movement in general, there were debates to do with the nature and purpose of pornography and prostitution and the camps were sometimes divided. Beverley Harrison was among those who alerted us to the 'pornographic mindset' which she saw as active in the objectifying stance of much male theology as she did in the porn industry itself. This insight has been valuable for those reconsidering the place of pornography and the way in which the systems under which we operate may not be as far apart as they appear; they may indeed simply be varying manifestations of the patriarchal mindset. Feminists have always defended the right of women to work in prostitution, but with the increase in sex-trafficking and the huge exploitation of children within the area as well as the increasing evidence, medical and social, regarding this way of life, there is cause to reflect again.

Many of these debates have arisen again in the light of the impact of queer theory on feminist theology. The postmodern agenda makes it imperative that we look with new eyes at the old questions, and especially in the light of rethinking what it is that women may be that we do not come to easy and safe answers – sexual theology asks that we be bold in order to fully explore the depths of our human–divine nature. If Heyward is right, and we believe she is, then it is in the depth of our relationality, a relationality that is tested, stretched and enabled through skin-on-skin engagement, that we find the depth of the divine. Incarnation is not for the faint-hearted!

Of course there is a difference between not being faint-hearted and actually being blind to some of the old ways creeping in under another and seemingly more inclusive name. In the acceptance and positive embracing of a range of sexual preference, feminist theology has done much to make people's lives more liveable and to see more fully the scope and nature of the divine. There are those, however, who worry that this all-embracing agenda should have limits. Although Sheila Jeffreys' is not a theologian, she is an activist with a keen eye for the pitfalls lurking in sexuality and gender. She is concerned that in considering gender as a performance we are still stuck within binary opposites when looking for ways to perform; and that in perhaps being afraid to question such things as butch/femme relationships and transsexual surgery we are reinforcing all that we say we have stood against for years – that is, the binary opposition of male and female and the unequal power structure that it enables. She is concerned that a number of older butches are opting for surgery as their bodies soften and they look more female: in order to overcome this they go under the knife. Jeffreys is understandably concerned that both womanhood and lesbianism are being undermined here in an attempt to opt into male power and privilege.[32] She is also aware that when academic language is used and sexuality is spoken of in academic language it becomes difficult to criticize without being labelled as out of touch. She ventures to suggest that much butch/femme role-playing popularizes a watered-down form of S&M in which dominance and submission are embraced as delights and not political problems.[33] So we see that even with the gains of the feminist discourse, there remain many areas to be cautious about when approaching. Do we have to ask why, for example, women find pleasure in inflicting pain? Can we be content with the old assurance that this is a bad habit learnt under years of patriarchal rule, or do we have to look deeper and face some very disquieting realities?

If it was ever believed that opening up the sacredness of female sexuality would be an easy path, then time has proved otherwise. There has been, as we may have expected, a great deal of backlash from the churches, but the path has not been smooth within the discipline itself. While many have welcomed this development, there have been others who have seen it as another way of reinforcing the relationship between the nature of women and sexuality in a less than positive way. In addition, concern was voiced through the Good Sex project that western values were once again to the forefront when the reality of many women's lives, particularly in the East, was that sex was far from a blessing let alone a place of sacred meaning. Those who are in the sex trade that serves western consumerism were felt to have no voice in this discourse, while those from religions such as Buddhism felt that this was a Christian dialogue that took little account of other ideas of the body. At the time of the project it was also felt that little, if any, attention had been paid to the notion of celibacy. Although I was not the first to do so, we can now reply that it has been addressed[34] and with some seriousness, albeit as a sexual stance. While we welcome the critique

32 Sheila Jeffreys, *Unpacking Queer Politics*, Polity, 2003, p. 130.

33 Jeffreys, *Unpacking Queer Politics*, p. 127.

34 Isherwood, *Power of Erotic Celibacy*.

from other religions and accept that it is from within those systems that statements have to be made about the nature of female sacred sexuality, we are more defensive over the idea that when speaking of sexuality there was no acknowledgement that women are exploited in this area. There has always been a keen awareness that women are situated differently and that this contextuality hugely affects all matters to do with the divine through the lived reality of women. We accept the differences and acknowledge that feminist theologians need to tread carefully when they open areas for discussion.

An interesting challenge has also been offered form the other side of the debate so to speak. Marcella Althaus-Reid calls liberation theologies to task for not having the honesty to face the full reality of women's lives.[35] She claims that much liberation theology, of which the feminist sexual theology was a part, can only deal with 'decent women', that is to say with those who are seen as suffering and sexually pure. The married mother who is the victim of domestic abuse is within the remit but the poor woman who likes sex, all kinds of transgressive and beyond the pale sex, is a test for feminist liberation theology. Her experience is not included within the lived reality of women and men which helps us expand theological horizons. Althaus-Reid points out that the experiences of many women are not included in the activity of feminist sexual theology and she urges a new look and a move beyond. She questions whether queer theology is the next step that we have to take if we really are to include the experiences of the prostitute, the mistress and the dominatrix in the outworking of sexuality and the sacred. This is a set of questions that make many very uncomfortable and particularly when there is a christological challenge embedded in the questioning.[36] Althaus-Reid is right, if we are declaring the sacredness of female sexuality it is counterproductive to place a ring around the good sex and the bad sex, feminist theologians have to get far more comfortable with sex,

---

35 Marcella Althaus-Reid, *Indecent Theology: Theological Perversions in Sex, Gender and Politics*, London: Routledge, 2001.

36 See Chapter 4 of this book.

all kinds of sex, and not run and hide behind the gender discourse.[37] Incarnation is much rawer than that!

So raw, in fact, that it is constantly challenging the edges of any discourse in theology. In the area of sexuality it does seem that there is tension in feminist theology particularly over whether the discipline can carry forward the harder questions. There is a more disturbing notion though and that is that sexuality is once again a private matter, one that is concerned with integrated, happy people doing whatever gives them pleasure. Feminist theology for these people has helped to make sexuality a broader playing field and contributed to the political move for more rights and the social movement for more acceptances regarding a range of sexual preferences. This is alarming since the political goes much deeper than this; in our opinion we would do well to keep the words of Heyward in front of us when she said, 'When I say I love you, let the revolution begin'. This is no statement of simple self-acceptance and contentment; it is a fundamental declaration of the personal as political and a commitment to embodied justice-seeking between two people and far beyond into the whole social order. It is the kind of revolution that is spoken of in the Song of Songs where the lovers challenge all convention, race, class, economics, and place their sex (there is very little mention of love and certainly no marriage envisaged) within the widest possible context, that of the cosmos itself as an act of revolution.[38] One of the authors of this book believes feminist theology cannot encompass all that is needed to take sexual theology all the way, it still works in binaries and thus creates borderlands and boundaries. The other believes the truly radical nature of incarnation has not yet been explored by feminist theologians, who she thinks have most of the tools needed to go further, what is lacking is passion and courage. How appropriate this is and how empowering for the continuing debate!

---

37 See Lisa Isherwood, 'Indecent Theology: What F…ing Difference Does it Make', in *Feminist Theology*, Vol. 11.2 (January 2003), pp. 141–7.

38 See Lisa Isherwood, '"Eat, Friends, Drink. Be Drunk with Love" (Song of Songs 5.2): A Reflection', in *Patriarchs, Prophets and Other Villains*, L. Isherwood (ed.), London: Equinox, forthcoming.

2

Myths Surrounding Feminist
Theological Hermeneutics

What we do differently and why

This incident occurred a few years ago: I was attending a conference of Latinas doing theology in the USA when I saw a young woman walking down an aisle of the conference room. On her t-shirt were the following words: 'I'm not a Latina. I am Mexican, thank you!' As the conference progressed, with important presentation papers and discussions on the different tranches of Latino/a theology, hispanas doing theology and mujeristas, a friend sitting beside me confided that she did not identify herself within the title mujerista theology,[1] or feel comfortable with it. She would rather be known as a Latina theologian in the United States. On other occasions, I have seen how important was the mujerista identity for many women. In any case, this was not the first time that I sensed that the differences and dis-

---

1 Mujerista is a style of doing theology for Latinas in the United States which comes from the Cuban theologian Ada Maria Isasi Diaz. It is based on a specific ethnographic methodology and has a strong ethical perspective. The term 'mujerista' comes from the Spanish 'mujer' (woman). Latino/a is a theology represented by Maria Pilar Aquino, among others, also in the United States. Hispanas is a term used as exchangeable for mujerista and Latina but it tends to refer to a more specific Roman Catholic type of theology (hispano theology), although there are also Protestant developments. The term 'hispano' is in itself controversial. Many Latin Americans would not like to have their identities linked to a nomenclature which comes from the Conquista and refer to an European ethnic claim instead of their own Original Nations.

agreements among Latinas and mujeristas (or in the case just mentioned, Latinas vs Mexicans) reflected somehow the reality of the differences among Latin Americans by birth or by family ties in the United States. Such differences are not necessarily grounded in their church or denominational backgrounds or in specific doctrinal disputes, or in issues of church structures. They seem to have far deeper roots, connected with the way women construct their own identities. Why, for example, have womanists (Black American theologians) never engaged in any serious theological project with black Brazilian women, or with indigenous women from the many non-white communities of Latin America? After all, for all of them race constitutes their hermeneutical circle. Or again, why is it that women from the large cities of developing world countries tend to become excluded from the mostly peasant-based feminist theological debates? To put it another way, city prostitutes in Sao Paulo or Buenos Aires are also poor women, but they are not necessarily represented in the discourse of liberation theologies.

Although feminist theology represents in itself a long theological detour in search of female identity, paradoxically, our differences related to doing feminist theologies seem to arise from issues concerning precisely the way we construct our identities. It is not so much who we sense we are (culturally and historically) but that the frameworks we use to construct our identities differ, not just in terms of gender, but of class, race and sexuality. What we question and to what depth we interrogate hermeneutically, are always ideologically loaded issues. Theological honesty requires from us the acknowledgement that although we have been asking ourselves many questions over the last four decades, we have also presupposed more homogeneity in our constructions of female identity than we should. Not surprisingly we have now come to realize that we are less in agreement than we previously thought. For instance, Mujeristas and Latinas may represent Latin-based communities of women in the USA, but they are not necessarily addressing themselves to the same constituencies. The differences between first-generation American (or second or even third) and those born in Latin America can reflect not only different experiences but also national allegiances. Or perhaps we have to recognize that indeed social being determines consciousness. We might ask ourselves if being a woman (a gender locus) is more important for the construction of female identity than being of a certain race. Some years ago a Dutch womanist theologian shared with me her experience that when she walked in the street in Amsterdam, the colour of her skin was more decisive for her own identity than was her gender. She could hear people commenting 'here comes a black woman': her womanhood was only a secondary and less important aspect of how society perceived her. A related example concerns womanists who are black American women. Within America it is their race which determines their identity, but in relation to developing world women it may well be their nationality which determines their identity and their political and theological allegiances. Alice Walker, the founder of womanist theory, is a case in point. She tells of a visit some years ago to Cuba. On meeting a group of school children of a wide spectrum of colours, she introduced herself as a *black* American. The children were confused: they had not thought of themselves in terms of colour. In this context Walker came to see the term 'black' as a 'perverted categorization'.[2] She also met with Cuban women, who understood themselves to be part of the Cuban socialist revolution, not an American feminist revolution. For Brazilian women, what the USA represents in the history of their nation and the life of their communities may be a crucial factor in forming their identities. Even I myself, an Argentinian woman of unusually pale, white colour of skin, have been challenged about my Latin American identity by women who construct identities in terms of dark skin colour.

These examples help us to understand the complexity of the construction of identity in feminist theologies. There are of course many further issues to be taken into account. Women who live in countries

---

2 Alice Walker, *In Search of Our Mothers' Gardens*, London: The Women's Press, 1994, p. 212. See also Alistair Kee *The Rise and Demise of Black Theology*, Aldershot: Ashgate, 2006, p. 109.

where Christianity is a minority religion work with frameworks of plurality and inclusiveness. This has been the context for many Asian theologians. And, of course, not all women are women in accordance with the ideological sexual definitions of womanhood: there is more to being a woman than being born one. The sexual paradigm has opened windows upon worlds we have not always acknowledged. In the light of all this we have to ask whether there are any patterns that we can identify in conflicts and controversies. Or is it true that in feminist theology the pattern is one of dialogue and inclusiveness, based on a common feminist hermeneutical circle? It is true that the twenty-first century has seen issues of identity become increasingly contentious in the discourse of Feminist theologies, particularly with regard to gender and sexuality, but it has been claimed that feminist theologies do have a common hermeneutical style, which can accommodate differences and tensions while working within the same framework of action and reflection. Let us first consider briefly the way that the hermeneutical circle of feminist theologies works, and how its different elements relate to each other.

Current myths of feminist hermeneutics

Theology is an interpretative art: we interpret the scriptures, the traditions of our churches and more importantly, the kairos in which we live and give our Christian prophetic testimony. Feminist theologies have contributed to a particular hermeneutical style of action–reflection–action, but one of the most accepted myths surrounding feminist theologies has been the idea that, no matter where the theologians were actually coming from, they have always had a commonality in their methodology. That methodology has usually been described as praxis. It starts with the experience of women in order to provide the grounding for a theological reflection which aims to transform the life conditions of women in church and in society. Let us take, for instance, the important contribution of Elizabeth Schüssler Fiorenza in this area, which together with that of

Rosemary Radford Ruether has been formative in the developing of the liberationist hermeneutics of suspicion in feminist theology. In her book *Wisdom Ways*[3] Schüssler Fiorenza has developed one of the most comprehensive feminist hermeneutical frameworks, based on her own experience and that of other theologians working in the area over a period of more than four decades. The result is impressive and even a cursory reading of this work will demonstrate the argument that there is a commonality of hermeneutical approach which can be appropriated by theologians from different backgrounds, traditions and cultural expectations. It consists of four related elements:

1 A hermeneutics of suspicion
2 A hermeneutics of proclamation
4 A hermeneutics of remembrance
5 Creative actualization

Anyone familiar with liberationist hermeneutics will actually recognize in this the different elements of a framework of interrogating ideological stances. Suspicion is represented by the questioning of the taken-for-granted, thus ideologically accepted. Proclamation refers to a process of denounciation and annunciation with regard to the structures of sin prevalent in churches and societies. Remembrance is more specific than in liberationist hermeneutics. It is the moment to inscribe in the theological reflection the memories of the women of the past, both from the scriptures but also from the invisible history of the church. Finally, all these moments of reflection are to be brought together in a resolution, a praxis, which symbolizes the changing and transformative character of feminist hermeneutics. The differences have always been considered to be of a thematic nature, but those themes may be informed from different perspec-

---

3 See Elisabeth Schüssler Fiorenza, *Wisdom Ways: Introducing Feminist Biblical Interpretation*, New York: Orbis, 2001. In this text, Fiorenza has combined different contextual interpretative frameworks with the Hebrew Wisdom literature as a hermeneutical clue.

tives, for instance cultural, or political. However, we wish to claim that there are profound divisions concerning symbolic patterns of understanding Christianity, including the place or lack of it of the scripture in feminist hermeneutics. Let us see in more detail now the controversies presented in the feminist hermeneutical circle.

Controversies in the hermeneutics of suspicion

The thematic controversy: politics or culture?

It would be naïve to suppose that feminist hermeneuticians differ in their themes or motives only according to their contexts. That would be equivalent to saying that the method is always the same, that we start with our experiences and produce relevant socio-economic and cultural analyses in order to develop a critical theological reflection pertinent to our context, the aim of which is the social transformation of gendered structures of oppression. Here we are confronted with the theme of the neutrality of the feminist theologian. First of all, let us reflect on the fact that the selection of themes is not a natural phenomena. One could argue that in feminist theology women's everyday experience is the criterion for the selection of themes which will serve as a thread to theological reflection. This is represented, for instance, in the criterion of *lo cotidiano* for Maria Pilar Aquino in her Latina theology; *la realidad* for Latin Americans; 'women's struggles' for Schüssler Fiorenza and Radford Ruether and the womanist experience for Delores Williams, to mention a few. However, how we select the relevant issues of every-day life, even of the history of women of our communities, is complex. There is, in fact, a split between choosing cultural or political issues, with a few who try to combine both reflecting the recent trend in theology to falsely oppose cultural to political hermeneutics. Some years ago I attended a conference in Sierra Leone, after the revolution. It was organized by the University of Edinburgh's Centre for the Study of World Christianity. A distinguished woman theologian from Africa, whom I admire, was quick to remark in the midst of a debate that 'Latin American women can do politics, but for Africans it is culture that counts.' This was said in the aftermath of Sierra Leone's bitter civil war. It deserved a deeper and broader discussion, but that was not possible at the time. The African theologians present (a male majority) were not interested and the western male theologians considered it to be 'an issue for women's discussion only'. The logic was that western theologians do not have a problem with becoming honorary Africans, but they would not participate in any theological reflection from the perspective of women. However, the split is further complicated with the coming of postcolonial theology. Musa Dube from South Africa (where the tradition of doing theology has been informed by the political struggle against apartheid) is one of the few African theologians to work with a complex methodology and thematic informed by issues of globalization as well with issues of gender in Africa.

Feminist Latin American theologians have in general been suspicious of postcolonial trends, but not of cultural hermeneutics. Some have argued that postcolonialism has been used to depoliticize otherwise political theologies, since the locus of reflection on power struggles tends to be reduced to discursive analysis. The Bible, or a novel by Conrad, could be the issue for a postcolonial analysis, showing the tensions and subversion inherent in colonial texts, but not necessarily the collapse of the banking system in Argentina in the twentieth century or a workers' strike. The reading of the Bible, which feminists have struggled to make accessible for women in relation to their experience, seems to have been taken away by postcolonial studies: there is no such a thing as 'popular postcolonial studies'. Yet some feminist theologians have managed to combine a liberationist and postcolonial approach which is knowledgeable and yet readable. Examples of theologians who have pioneered this area are Kwok Pui lan and Musa Dube. In Latin America, Nancy Cardoso Pereyra has developed a postcolonial political theology with reference to the realities of Brazilian popular religiosity among women. However, there are no theologies which encompass all the levels of political, economic, cultural, sexuality and gender and racial suspicion. Some tools of analysis are privileged over others. That in itself is symptomatic of other discrepancies in terms of feminist theology and identity, the sort of discrepancies which have led some feminist theologians historically to ask, 'Can a woman be a feminist and a Christian?' and others to question 'Can a woman be a Christian and a revolutionary?'

This produces, in fact, a further twist in the cultural versus cultural feminist theological paradigm, that is, how the theologian's identity is construed in relation to the presumed reader of her texts. For one thing, the relation of the theologian to her own culture is a disruptive one. Women do not usually come from a tradition of Christian women theologians and the cultural understanding of 'wise women' may differ significantly from the way we understand knowledgeable women. We should discuss this further in another moment of the hermeneutical circle, that is, the moment of remembering women from our communities. However, the theologian is somehow outside a culture, or at least we can say that she has an ambivalent relationship towards her own culture. It is from this cultural dislocation that she needs to produce a criticism of cultural practices which authorize women's oppression, and also the relationship between these cultural practices and Christian cultural ones. To this we need to add the fact that there is an increasing number of women theologians in diaspora, and the situations arising from the confrontation of different cultures and demands upon the communities of women in economic or political exile. The woman theologian herself may be part of a theological diaspora, for example because she has not been allowed to earn a living in her own country either by teaching, or as a minister of a church congregation. There are therefore different ways to construct the identity of a feminist theologian at the juncture of culture and politics. In fact the way that a cultural issue or a political crisis is highlighted in the feminist theological discourse may depend on the extent to which being a feminist or a revolutionary is more important for identity than being a Christian. The concept of 'action' or hermeneutics of transformation may depend on that also. The case of the Latinas in the USA is an interesting example. They are women concerned with political issues such as unemployment, immigration and racism. Yet they struggle with a cultural background which though relevant to their sense of identity may also conflict with possibilities of change. For many the political situation of Latin America is beyond their concern: they are Americans, fighting for their rights in their own country. For others, whose families are still in Latin America, there is serious concern for issues of US international policy.

On identity

One of the most persistent myths of feminist theologies has been the division between women theologians of the developing world and those of the western world, sometimes called 'white feminists', although the term does not necessarily apply in all cases. For a start the concept of race, as conceived and organized in US feminist discourses (including womanist) does not necessarily relate to the way race is understood among Latinas, Latin Americans and Caribbeans, or African or Asian women.

Any student who has not taken time to attend classes or read carefully the prescribed course material on feminist theologies would probably rush into affirming what I call the primordial myth of feminist theologies. This is a postcolonial point of reflection, the false separation and stereotyping of feminist theologies, which no doubt was not innocent of ideological intention. Let us consider this in detail. The primordial myth I am referring to asserts that feminist theologies were, or still are, divided into 'first world' and 'third world' categories. Following on from that was the assumption that 'first world' theologians were middle-class women preoccupied with academic issues, while 'third world' theologians were poor women preoccupied with the 'real issues' of women's lives. 'Real issues' in this context means questions concerning the economy, job markets, healthcare, the family and children. At times, and still in some evangelical circles, it was also assumed that feminist theologians of developing countries did not question theology and gender relationships, but had an agenda similar to that of men in the same situation of social injustice and oppression.

It was due to the influence of poor women (the mythical argument of the first–third world original divide continues) who were concerned with more important issues than the mere academic ones, that first world theologians changed their methodology and themes, or at least some of them did. This myth has been very pervasive: it can be found in church circles as in academic ones and it is surprising to still find comments and debates grounded in it. Although it is true that women theologians constantly influence and challenge each other, as the dialogue of feminist theology becomes more inclusive, the myth of white middle-class women versus the poor theologians must take some responsibility for the subsequent limited understanding of the differences surrounding the construction of women's identities in feminist theologies in general. To demonstrate that this division was never factual, we need only mention a well-known feminist theologian from the first generation, Rosemary Radford Ruether. She was a Roman Catholic theologian at Emory when she started her activism concerning issues of racial exclusion. She joined in solidarity with Latin American theologians during the difficult years of the dictatorial regimes, and produced a major difference in the way the pleas of Latin American theology (and women) were internationally received. Ruether was an active militant theologian at a time when few dared to be, including those living in Latin America.[4]

The truth however is paradoxical. While Radford Ruether was a role model of theology in action – and action since the 1970s – not every woman theologian of the developing world had the courage to defy not only the conventions of her society, the rules of her church,

---

4 Other examples of militant political feminists from the first generation of feminist theologians include Judith Plaskow, Ada Maria Isasi-Diaz, Delores Williams and Virginia Mollenkott in the United States. The first woman theologian from Latin America, Beatriz Melano Couch, was also a very militant, political theologian who confronted the military dictatorial regimes of the 1970s in Argentina.

the mores of her culture, but the structures of her teaching institution. Critical consciousness and political activism among feminist theologians cannot be automatically attributed to developing world women, even if in many cases it was justified. Therefore, we can say that feminist theology may be grounded in action, but theologians of the developing world do not have proprietary rights in the matter. In fact, the question of women's experience and theological reflection has been reduced at times to a point of fiction. How? Behind every piece of a feminist theological discourse there is an implicit reader community, lurking in the dark. These are imaginary communities of women readers, not because the women addressed are figments of the theologian's imagination, but because writing theology implies, to a certain extent, the construction of a symbolic identity, especially in times of globalization where geographical borders disappear and identities becomes a product of hybridization. However, feminist theology theologizes its subjects. Some time ago one of my students presented a proposal to write a dissertation based exclusively on a theology arising out of the story of a group of poor women. She envisaged challenges during her fieldwork, but also harmonic and creative lines for the developing of an 'authentic theology from ordinary women'. Months later, her disappointment was obvious: she found that the group of women she had researched seemed prone to repeat theological clichés without any questioning or understanding. Some were official church clichés, but others were feminist theological clichés. She asked me if there was any possibility of doing such a thing as a theology arising from women's everyday lives. In fact, she was questioning something she had erroneously assumed – that the protagonists of the theologies of the story have not been subject to a process of theologization, that is, the role of the feminist theologian in organizing and rereading women's experiences in church and in society.

48

Symbols

How can feminist theologians be creative, finding a way to a liberative praxis, and yet be entrapped by masculinist language, metaphors and more crucially, Christian male symbolism? Important theological lines have been divided upon this point, which also has links to the old question: 'Can a woman be a feminist and a Christian?' Leaving aside the fact that the adjective 'feminist' is complex enough because, as we have already seen it covers different 'waves of thinking'. Historically these have included opposite viewpoints, such as struggles for equality or for difference, reform or radical change. Feminism cannot but question Christian symbols. Latin American feminists have done that through their cultural and sometimes political readings. Thus Elsa Támez provided us with an early example of intertextual symbolic system reading by reflecting on the Bible from a Mexican myth of origins.[5] Womanists have done the same, as when Dolores Williams pioneered a reading of the story of Hagar together with the socioeconomic realities of black women in the USA. The theme of Hagar in relation to domestic workers was also successfully worked by Támez in Latin America.

Symbolic intertextuality has been well-developed in feminist theologies. Just to mention a few examples, (Chung) Hyun Kyung[6] in a Korean context and Mercy Oduyoye in Ghana[7] have shown the

5 Cf. Elsa Támez's article, 'Introduction: The Power of the Naked' in E. Támez (ed.), *Through Her Eyes: Women's Theology from Latin America*, New York: Orbis, 1989.

6 (Chung) Hyun Kyung's first book, *Struggle to Be the Sun Again: Introducing Asian's Women Theology*, New York: Orbis, 1990, dealt with issues of enculturation, politics and the challenges of a Korean multifaith society. Some of her more recent work, which comes from her experience becoming a Buddhist monk is more goddess-centred and ecological. See, for instance, her four volumes entitled *Goddess-Spell According to Hyung Kyung: A Letter from Goddess to the Earth and Keeping Women Warriors of the World*, Pa-Yu: Yolimwon, 2001. She has recently decided not to continue using her father's surname Chung.

7 Mercy Oduyoye is a pioneer Ghanaian theologian and author of many books including *Daughters of Anowa: African Women and Patriarchy*, New York: Orbis, 1995.

complexities of this type of reflection. The work of Chung is interesting because of its pedagogical implications. In fact, Chung could
not keep the 'balance' that cultural hermeneutics seems to require,
and she had good reason for that. The search for symbolic balance
betrays a colonial hermeneutical imposition. With the years, Chung
has moved towards a strong female spiritual symbolic which is
related to the goddesses reflections or thealogy. The controversy
here relates to how deep into a female cultural symbolic can a
theologian go without compromising the integrity of a hermeneutical circle which is supposed to be rooted in women's experiences? It
must be said that feminist theology has been born from the experience of women theologians and church activists. We are not talking
here of women who could organize their experiences outside theological and ecclesiastical boundaries, but women who tended to
theologize their own and other women's experiences in their
church community. Somehow that is the controversial kernel of the
'theology of the story', for to do theology in community, as women,
and from our experiences, has meant sometimes to teach women to
theologize their experience, that is, to produce a symbolic balance
between female and patriarchal universes. In this Hyung Kyung
followed that pioneer theologian, Carol Christ, and also the writings
from the influential Naomi Goldenberg.[8] Somehow it seems that the

---

8 Carol Christ is a pioneer theologian who currently lives in Greece and
organizes goddess workshops for women. Christ wrote a very influential article
entitled, 'Why Women Need the Goddess' in the journal *Heresies: The Great
Goddess Issue* (1978), reprinted in C. Christ and J. Plaskow *Womanspirit
Rising: A Feminist Reader on Religion*, San Francisco: Harper and Row, 1979.
Among her many books, *Laughter of Aphrodite: Reflections on a Journey to the
Goddess*, San Francisco: Harper and Row, 1987 has been printed many times
and it is considered a classic theological textbook.

Naomi Goldenberg is a psychoanalyst and theologian whose first book
entitled *Changing the Gods: Feminism and the End of Traditional Religion*,
Boston: Beacon Press, 1979. This book had a tremendous influence on many
feminist theologians and contributed to a shifting of paradigms from patriarchal
constructions of God towards a more authentic feminist imaginary of the
sacred. Goldenberg has published extensively in this area.

first wave of the feminist theological hermeneutical movement had a radical enquiry about female symbolism but divided into two different trends; as some women were working in female spirituality, others wanted to rescue female symbolism suppressed in patriarchal Christianity and also Judaism. The radical reading into Judeo-Christian female spirituality somehow became normative for future generations of theologians, although it did not need to be that way. This is a theme that has been long debated in the corridors of feminist theological conferences. There is an area of female spirituality which is elusive though, and there are many theologians who find that a female spirituality requires less labelling and much more honesty. In fact, the accusations of these theologians to the rest has been why they did not develop theological research more in tune with elements which are from women and which challenge the idea of rediscovering the feminine face of God among patriarchal Christian discourses.

However, the confrontation of the thealogian versus feminist theologians does not reflect the state of the art in the twenty-first century because the overcoming of the sexual paradigm over the gender one has produced a further diversification in the debate, represented by those who want to deconstruct heterosexuality more than patriarchy. The sexual suspicion has had consequences for the goddess or theological paradigm. The old suspicion returns, that even goddess cults have been located in the midst of patriarchal cultures, now that the suspicion of heterosexual construction into the goddesses is added.[9]

Controversies in proclamation

Issues concerning identity are the most important in the feminist hermeneutical circle. In fact they precede and deeply influence the

---

9 See for instance the *Journal of Feminist Theology* 1 (2005); vol. 13, dedicated to the current evaluation of the goddess movement and theological research.

other elements of the hermeneutical enquiry, particularly the step of proclamation. Proclamation, following Schüssler Fiorenza, refers to the moment of properly reading the scriptures, while evaluating how the scriptures relate to the situation of contemporary women.[10] That in itself has been contested on grounds of identity, as some early theologians considered that the Bible with its patriarchal tradition cannot be a source of spiritual authority for women. Furthermore, the use of the scriptures may tacitly deny women's own sources of spirituality and contradict their experiences. Daphne Hampson and Mary Daly[11] are examples of theologians who challenge the validity of the scriptures for contemporary women and consider their use as an act of dishonesty for theologians professing to be feminists. The difficulties regarding the use of the Bible have persisted, with even women theologians of developing countries (traditionally belonging to biblical theological traditions, such as the liberationists) expressing their doubts. Even Támez expressed the view during the 1980s that the suspicion fell not on the use of the texts (the traditional patriarchal exegesis), but on the process of writing and assembling the collection of texts we call the Bible. After Phyllis Trible's *Texts of Terror* (1984)[12] and the works of other theologians which denounced the politics of violence and dehumanization advocated

10 Schüssler Fiorenza, *Wisdom Ways*, 'Introduction', pp. 1–12.

11 Both Daly and Hampson were considered 'postChristian' theologians, who left Christianity but in the case of Hampson, without joining the thealogical movement, yet continuing research in God and spirituality. Hampson's most influential book was *Theology and Feminism*, Oxford: Blackwell, 1990 (reprinted several times). Mary Daly has many influential books characterized by a very radical stance not only theologically but from the perspective of how a woman theologian should write. See, for instance, her widely influential early text *Beyond God the Father*, Boston: Beacon Press, 1993 which still remains original and highly provocative.

12 Phyllis Trible, *Texts of Terror: Literary-Feminist Readings of Biblical Narratives*, Minneapolis: Ausburg Fortress Publishers, 1984 was one of the first books to challenge the principle that every text from the Bible could be successfully reread from a feminist perspective.

in the scriptures, it was necessary to apply a criterion in relation to the reading of the scriptures. That criterion was a liberationist one which Latin American theologians called 'the use of the radical principle'. In practice it means that one needs to exercise some selectivity in reading the scriptures, especially with texts which do not seem to be organized around principles such as social justice or the criteria of life as identified by developing world theologians. In Latin America this was called the biophilic principle, that is, the principle of life and elements pro-life surrounding a text. A vengeful, blood-thirsty, biblical god who is ready to personally destroy or require others to destroy whole nations, who remains silent at the rape and mutilation of women, says more about the community in which these texts were written and read than about the godself.

That third position has remained till now as the majority position among feminist theologians. Yet the late Grace Jantzen was not the only one to express her doubts about this principle of selective biblical authority, while objecting to the patriarchal milieu of the scriptures.[13] If the Bible was to be considered non-normative, why then read it, and why spend so much time and energy in order to make a sensible use of a patriarchal, non-normative theological source? The debate still continues, but there are women who do biblical interpretation in order to work with sacred texts which are very relevant to many women. That has been Schüssler Fiorenza's intention, and she is not alone in that. However, the issue of theological identity haunts this second moment of the hermeneutical circle, when other women ask if the theologian is herself engaged in a biblical exercise for the sake of a community, even if she does not sense its validity anymore. Some years ago, while attending a conference, I had a conversation with a feminist theologian of world-renown who confessed her disillusion with the reading of the scriptures among the community of women. She did not foresee any radical change of consciousness arising in the church and in

---

13 Cf. Grace Jantzen, 'Sources of Religious Knowledge', in Literature and Theology, Vol. 10.2 (June 1996), p. 14.

theology concerning women from what she called a 'limited' exercise of reading and mending the Bible. When I challenged her, asking why she continued publishing and doing community work in this area, she clearly separated herself from her community: she felt that for many simple Christian women that was enough to help them on a daily basis. That, in itself, relates to Schüssler Fiorenza's claims that the reading of the scripture should continue as we cannot ignore the communities of Christian women for whom the Bible is an instrument of oppression and yet who are deeply religious women who need to find something else in the scriptures. Moreover, they need to have the right to wrestle with the scriptures. After all, it is more positive to wrestle with the scriptures, sensing that one is wrestling with God, than with dry church encyclicals and documents.

The issue of proclamation is to work around a scriptural agreement on the authority of God in the texts, but not in all the texts. Processes of deideologization similar to the ones used by liberation theologians have been used. If anything, they tend to uncover a greater and more admirable God, and in this sense, feminist hermeneuticians have contributed much more than others to the validation of the scriptures in our times. The second aspect of the moment of proclamation forces us to think about the context of the second part of the proposition concerning the validity of the Bible for contemporary women. For instance, Latin American women have discovered the Bible in recent decades, and although the traditional Catholic Church in the continent does have a past of oppressive interpretation and use of the scriptural texts against women, the Latin Americans have felt in general empowered by the fact that they could actually read those texts and dispute their interpretation. For women of Asian traditions such as Kwok Pui Lan[14]

---

14 Kwok Pui-Lan is a pioneer scholar who had advanced the research area of postcolonialism, gender studies and religion. See, for instance, her book, *Postcolonial Imagination and Feminist Theology*, Westminster: John Knox Press, 2005.

the challenge is to produce an interreligious hermeneutics, which includes the rediscovery of the Bible's own interreligious plural status. A similar process of broadening the canon seems to have been necessary for African women in hermeneutics. Why? Because women's religious everyday experiences cannot be cut free from their own cultural spiritual traditions. This is, in itself, part of a decolonization process in theology which needs to acknowledge the positive contribution of a hybrid hermeneutical circle.

The plurality and even mutual contradictions of women's experiences have been acknowledged and celebrated and nobody would claim a universal normative sense of identity and hermeneutical proclamation for women of diverse backgrounds. That itself is not problematic. What still is controversial is what has been perceived as lines of theological solidarity with women's different experiences and scriptural validation. In feminist theology to remain silent about other women's struggles is considered unethical. Yet women's interpretation of their realities varies politically and produces confrontations. For Palestinian women, struggling to read the scriptures not only in a patriarchal context, but in one where disputes about land issues are heavily fuelled by biblical readings, their hermeneutical questionings extend far beyond the Palestinian theological groups. Solidarity with them is not just political but also intellectual, since the intifada is seen as a contribution to western hermeneutics.[15] Liberal theologians may have different interests and even if disagreeing politically speaking, may not choose to openly enter into a debate about it. Curiously, the confrontations that we may expect at this stage are not always political disagreements but disagreements on priorities.

It is a well-known fact that women who gather to do theology from their stories, have expectations about the theological praxis which

---

15 For this point, see Judith G. Martin's, 'Liberating Palestinian Theology – The Need for a Contextual Spirituality', in Ursula King (ed.) *Spirituality and Society in the New Millennium*, Brighton: Sussex Academic Press, 2001, pp. 220–34.

may arise from a biblical study, which are very different from those of trained theologians. Their allegorical perception of the Bible may be related to the needs of emotional and economic survival. Women may identify themselves with male patriarchs, including dubious characters, if the main point of validation for the scriptural reading is, for instance, poverty, or the suffering of a people under political persecution. Every feminist theology develops around a theme or event which is considered more foundational than others and that event is a biblical narrative identified by its ability to converse with a crucial situation. Although feminist theologies tend to be inclusive in terms of analysis and thematic (for instance, gender, culture and race) in practice there is usually one element privileged over the rest. The idea of using the texts which converse with women's struggles today to feed our creativity in worship and liturgy has been successful. There has been agreement in the incorporation of different ways to convey a feminist theology beyond the written word, for instance through dance. Yet for some women it is difficult to escape stereotypes while dealing with women present in the Bible. In fact, many women today feel that they identify better with some male characters in the scriptures. Whenever in the past I have joined groups doing role-play and exploring texts from the Gospels, I have found that there were more women who could identify themselves with Peter than with the Virgin Mary. After all, Peter had doubts and was impulsive to the point of regretting his actions. However, he was a very human character and some women I met felt that for that reason they could identify themselves with him, but not with Mary whose unusual life marked by virginal conceptions and a son from God had little to do with their own.

Controversies in remembrance

The aim of this step is to integrate the past and present of what has been called the women church, that is, a community made of culturally diverse contemporary women who remember and honour their foremothers. This means that the suffering, injustices, even the silence of God and the churches, or the responsibility that the institution bears for women's oppression is not forgotten. There is also celebration for their achievements, their courage and the fact that somehow they are still present through our struggles. Remembering (as in re-membering, recreating the historical community of Christian women) has been given great importance in feminist hermeneutics. It is not just the recounting of events and deeds otherwise forgotten, but the way that feminist theologians reappropriate past struggles and also debates which have been relevant. By debates we do not mean necessarily theological discussions, but the understanding of what were the discussions, doubts and dilemmas faced by women in the church. For instance, the importance of the rereading of Genesis for debates about women's suffrage illustrates how hermeneutical paths have been forged by the need to contest the patriarchal state. The authority of the state works in a similar way to the traditional authority invoked by patriarchal theology: it lies in the past and it is built upon customs and traditions. Therefore remembrance in hermeneutics is a political action that works by dismantling the utopia of unity in traditions and uncontested norms. It demonstrates that gender and sexual discrimination do not have a point of origin but have been contested through history with different levels of success. For some theologians this means to confront issues raised by postcolonial theology, such as the struggle to acknowledge a past which is in conflict with Christianity. Among Latin American women this has drawn attention to the conflictive presence in the Americas of devotion to the Virgin Mary. For others the issues have been the extermination and demonization of our foremothers' religions.

For many women today, it is also the realization that although gender and sexuality have been contested sites in theology, there has been a wide spectrum in how seriously these matters have been taken in the churches and what changes have been produced. Sometimes older women feel that the women of the younger generations who are still committed to bring about changes (and the number may have decreased) are literally reinventing the wheel. The fact that we are still advocating a 'storytelling' theology, accompanied by a rereading of the scriptures based on a framework of multiple suspicions (of gender, class, sexuality, race and culture) is not necessarily a measure of our success, but rather of the failure of the institutional churches to seriously engage in a the debate about the power and control which underpin patriarchalism and theology. The other difficulty is related to conscientization processes. Women in the past may or may not have had the level of awareness required to interrogate the ideologies of gender and sexuality in the discourses of society and of the sacred. It may be that the same applies to women in biblical times. Critical consciousness about gender and sexuality cannot be expected at all times in all cultures. Therefore, women 're-membering' their ancestors may well be reinforcing stereotypes. Some feminist theologians advocate the wider use of awareness-raising and the sharing of critical tools of analysis in the same way that Carlos Mesters, the well-known popular Bible teacher among the poor in Brazil, thought it necessary to give classes in elementary Hebrew to the peasants. For women issues of gender and sexuality awareness are made more complicated by the continuous negotiation (especially among poor women) of codes regarding decency. The risks of exclusion for women already belonging to excluded groups are high and dangerous. The controversy here is focused around how much can be achieved by remembering the past. History tends to show that the churches do not capitalize on radical movements and have a tendency to discard approaches which in their own time were considered a new path.

There is also the problem of how a new praxis can be forged without raising awareness, and how remembrance can be used to specifically raise critical awareness. As an example of this I recall a coincidence. In 1999 the *Journal of Feminist Theology* published an article I wrote on queer theology and liberation theology (or 'indecent theology'). The article was called, 'On Wearing Skirts Without Underwear – Indecent Theology Challenging the Liberation Theology of the Pueblo'. By coincidence it was followed by an article by the African scholar Musimbi Kanyoro entitled, 'My Grandmother Would Approve: Engendering Gospel and Culture'. The two articles, printed side by side, represent two different positions. While 'On Wearing Skirts Without Underwear' advocates a rupture with the theological/ideological ingrained framework concerning gender and sexuality, 'My Grandmother Would Approve' stands for a critically based cultural reading of the gospel and church traditions in Africa. It would not be right to say that these positions are completely opposite, and yet I am certain that my own grandmother would have never approved of my theology. In the same way I have claimed elsewhere that if Chung has inflamed many theological vocations by claiming her desire to write a theology that her mother could understand, I have said that I would be suspicious if my mother understood my reflections. I should prefer to write a theology which could not be understood by women of the past, but which would be helpful in making sure that women in the future did not have to suffer as they did.

In many ways the controversy of being nurtured by the past, or of working in a position of rupture with it, varies in different combinations among feminist theologians. We should note that this is also reflected in the way women consider issues referring to the biblical canon. The consideration of having other sources of female wisdom is part of the need to do a theology nurtured by women's experiences, and Radford Ruether and Schüssler Fiorenza, among others, have seriously advocated the reading of texts which add to our understanding of God outside patriarchal experiences. As Fiorenza claims, remembrance is an act that makes us take positions around issues of normativity and exclusion; orthodoxy and heresy. Although acknowledging that it is right and necessary for feminist theologians to reclaim the sacredness of their experiences, historically dubbed as heretical, there has not been any interest in fixing new canons, nor in creating guidelines for the parallel readings of the scriptures. Many women tend to use texts from their own culture; others, texts from goddess worship but also examples of dance or poetical work which are significant for the life of a particular community. Some theologians do not use texts outside the Bible, and of course, not every feminist theologian is a biblical specialist. What is important is that women's countertraditions are well-located, but even so some of these traditions are still too close to patriarchal Christianity and reformist attitudes instead of mounting serious challenges to the system.

Creative actualization

Feminist theologies claim to be theologies of praxis, that is, of action–reflection–action. Their criterion of veracity is to be found in the challenging and eventual transformation of structures of religious oppression. Instead of asking, 'What have you read?', the question has usually been, 'How have you acted?' In this way the hermeneutical circle proves to be non-linear, as the moment of action is also a moment in which women remember and evaluate the action of other women in sometimes similar situations. Creative actualizations have given place to many social movements and initiatives, yet they have never produced a 'women church', that is an ecclesiastical space organized solely under feminist understandings of structures and relationships. Instead of that, the 'women church' has been developed only as a conceptual umbrella for the fostering of relationships of solidarity and networking among women from different church affiliations. Issues of identity and particularly of church identity seem to be crucial in determining a feminist biblical process of interpretation and action. The controversies among feminist theologians that we find at this stage could have been envisaged at the beginning of the circle.

The fact is that in order to produce actions of transformation in the lives of women, many feminist theologians moved away from church activism and became involved in social projects including those dealing with issues of domestic abuse, land, unemployment and health. Some women felt that to produce any kind of relevant actions it was better to do it outside the church, where the possibilities of negotiating gender and sexual worldviews may be less demanding than in church circles. It may be said that the best of the work done for women usually happens at the margins of the church, where it is easier to find consensus around issues of social justice without the need to justify them theologically. There are also possibilities of alliances outside the churches with men and other groups also struggling for issues of justice and peace resolution. However, the fact that women cannot, or find it difficult to, construct a church identity outside their inherited traditions shows that the possibilities of transforming the church are limited. There are still women who think that by serving on church committees and maintaining a presence they may be able to influence the organization of the church. This may be possible, but other women think that it takes too long and are conscious of the tendency already referred to of the setting aside of radical alternative paths: allowing them to function within the church may be a way of marginalizing and controlling their efforts for change.

The women's ordination movement is a good example. Most churches have accepted the ordination of women, but many women feel unhappy by the lack of support in their work. If the structures which regulate power in the churches are not modified by the simple presence of women in ministerial roles, then changes are slow to happen. Without a critical debate about just what is intended in ordination there is always the danger that women clergy reinforce the very features of power and authority to which feminists object.

Finally, the main question which remains in dispute is what kind of changes or actions for transformation are envisaged for the last part of the feminist hermeneutical circle. For many women, changes in the church structures and theological thinking are not important anymore: they aim to produce collective actions for the affirmation and solidarity of women. The 'principle of life' or biophilic principle that we have already discussed is the focus of the biblical exercises among women. This we have seen flourishing in women's Ming Jung compounds in Korea and in Ecclesial Base Communities in

Latin America. We can see this among many women's groups and movements throughout the world, including the women of the African Circle of Theological Concern and in the many womanist, mujerista, Latina, lesbian or queer circles. Yet some women argue that this could be done without having a link with the church or the Bible: women's groups sharing experiences and helping each other have always existed. In fact, adding theology to discussions concerning how to resolve everyday struggles could become a further burden to distract women from their main goals. For others, the influence of Christianity in sexual and gender-identity formation, and the part it plays in the maintenance of traditional social, political and familial relations require critical reflection. At least for those societies and cultures still deeply influenced by the churches at legal and civil levels there will be no significant changes without an understanding of how religious institutions operate at an ideological level.

The different perspectives and even contradictions found among feminist theologians have not been a sign of weakness, but rather evidence of the strength and resilience of the movement. Women have had the courage to interrogate their own work at the most fundamental level, without taking anything for granted. In that sense, to have different positions and even to change the way we think over the years, have been among the most positive features of feminist theology. How we would have failed if the movement had been characterized by the patriarchal virtues of unity, uniformity and orthodoxy rather than dialogue, exchange and reflexivity! It was when the waters of the pool of Bethesda were troubled that the Spirit of God drew near.

3

The Virgin Mary: Many Images, Many Interests

In the course of one of her last visits to Great Britain I invited the late Uruguayan theologian Maria Teresa Porcile Santiso to give a seminar to a group of students of feminist theology in the School of Divinity in Edinburgh, Scotland. Porcile Santiso agreed and presented a paper about one of her specialities, female spirituality in Latin America. It was in this framework that she engaged with the theme of the Virgin Mary, and the developments of Mariology in the continent. After her presentation, students wanted to further discuss her paper, especially the controversies surrounding the place of the Virgin Mary in Latin American feminist theology. Could Mary become a liberator, or the 'guerrilla mother' (as in some Asian theological approaches, particularly in the Philippines, she has been represented)? Was not Mariology associated with *Marianismo*, that is the strict gender codes which regulate the life of women in Latin America? They wanted to know more about the debates in the approach to this theme. Porcile Santiso, who was a lay Catholic theologian, agreed that these were some of the areas of contention concerning Mary in her continent, but there were more crucial ones. To illustrate her point she shared the fact that she has found women who seemed not to believe that the Virgin of Guadalupe has really appeared to an indigenous man called Juan Diego. Moreover, she added, some believe that the cloth (which is said to have a 'divine imprint' of the Virgin's likeness) was a fraud. Porcile Santiso was aghast, but confessed that there were theologians who did not believe in the miraculous apparitions, so dear to Latin American women in general. It was at that moment I discovered that for Porcile Santiso among other theologians, Mariology was a question of belief in divine apparitions. That was the basic line. It was no ancient Palestine and the reading of the Gospels, but Guadalupe in Mexico and miraculous appearances which attracted her attention and theological reflections. Yet in the theology of liberation Christology has never been dependent on belief in any miraculous apparition or sacred objectification among Latin American theologians. On the contrary, liberation theologians have produced new metaphors for Christ far beyond medieval European imaginations. Therefore there was the Christ guerrillero, and the Christ worker in a factory. Christ was imagined wearing a miner's helmet or joining the queue of unemployed men in the city. Christ was contextualized, but the belief in the holy imprinted cloth was not considered a relevant element here. Liberationists believed in Christ by believing in Christ's project of the kingdom of God or the alternative society, not by believing in some latter-day supposed printing of his face on a cloth. Yet, Mariology, especially in the developing world context, seems to have revolved around two basic concepts. One concerns purely the belief in the narratives and legends of Marian apparitions, and the other concerns the relationship of Mary to patriotic causes. Nationalism and Mariology seem to have gone hand in hand in many developing countries. Unfortunately, military dictatorial regimes have always been Marian-based as well. Belief in the apparitions and 'belief' in the cause of one's country seem to have been at the root of Mariology in Latin America and also in the context of the Philippines.

From this perspective Mariology becomes a highly charged emotional area where discussions are not always possible because there are cultural identity elements and affective issues behind the discourse. There is no doubt that the rediscovery of Mary in liberation theologies in general and feminist theologies in particular has been an empowering event in the lives of many women in developing countries. They suddenly found that Marian devotion did not need to contradict their desire for gender and socioeconomic justice. On the contrary, they found that Mary could liberate them and the whole church from oppressive patriarchal ideologies. However, in other contexts, women have had the opposite experience. It was Mary Daly who denounced the image of Mary as symbolically dangerous for women, perpetuating sexual submission and even legitimatizing rape.[1] Daphne Hampson also followed this line as she considered how for many centuries Mariology has created and perpetuated ideals of submission and gender role stereotypes among women.[2] Mariology does play a role, for example, in episodes of domestic violence, when the women experience difficulty in asserting themselves over against a submissive role. However, feelings of guilt through disobedience are more properly related to cultural patriarchal affective patterns in general, including family relations, than to Mariology. For Hampson, the symbol of Mary is irredeemable. Yet, historically, it is also true that women may have been privately subverting the patriarchal construction of Mary in order to survive in a patriarchal church and society.

There is clearly a disagreement and dispute here, but if feminist theology claims the right of women to do theology from their own experience, both arguments in favour or against Mariology should somehow be respected. For some women, the implications of the construction of Mary's identity as biological (although defective) is an obstacle that can not be surmounted. The defectiveness of Mary as a biological woman is, by the way, no small obstacle for many theologians. They see in the Virgin Mary the culmination of the pollution laws of ancient Israel, embodied in a female–divine without menstruation, intercourse or in a 'polluted' act of giving birth.[3]

---

1 Cf. Mary Daly, *Gyn/Ecology: The Metaethics of Radical Feminism*, Boston: Beacon Press, 1990, p. 75.

2 Cf. Daphne Hampson, *After Christianity*, London: SCM Press, 1996, pp. 175–6.

3 Daphne Hampson wrote: 'In the 4th century the idea came to prominence that Mary's hymen had remain intact through the birth of Jesus . . . Mary's *in partu* virginity was an issue addressed by all the great theologians of the period' (Hampson, *After Christianity*, p. 189).

Women have been asked by their churches to follow Mary, to be good mothers and, above all, to be feminine by being passive and obedient to their husbands. The myth of virginity introduced into Christianity with Mariology may well have damaged many generations of women living in contexts in which virginity has acquired a disproportionately high commodity value. A whole strand of Christian ethics has been based on the objectification of women's bodies and sexuality. From there, it is easy to understand the continuing objectification of women in Christian cultures and in their legal systems. Yet, for some theologians such as Hyung Kyung or Vuola,[4] the virginity of Mary can be interpreted as a very revolutionary act.

Hyung Kyung represents a line of feminist theology in which virginity is not interpreted as a passive element in the construction of Mariology. On the contrary, it can be understood as the liberation of women from patriarchalism. Mary's virginity empowers her and gives her independence. To support this idea, I found a comment in the *Biblia Latinoamericana* (Latin American Bible) which elaborates the same concept – but for Christian men. Attention is drawn to Matthew 1.18: 'Now the birth of Jesus Christ took place in this way. When his mother Mary had been betrothed to Joseph, before they came together she was found to be with child of the Holy Spirit.' The comment then follows. 'How many men may feel anxious after reading this page! Can we say that God does not need men? Precisely, this is the point. There is no place for [a human father].'[5] While the text also deals with the empowerment element that virginity symbolizes for Mary in the patriarchal society of New Testament times, the commentators emphasize also the challenge that the text presents to masculinity. They go on to add a word of reassurance to

---

4 Elina Vuola is a Finnish theologian specializing in Latin American feminist theology. She has done extensive research on Mariology. See, for instance, her book *Limits of Liberation: Feminist Theology and the Ethics of Poverty and Reproduction*, London: Continuum, 2002.

5 Cf. Ramón Ricciardi and Bernardo Hurault, *El Nuevo Testamento: La Biblia Latinoamericana*, Madrid: Verbo Divino, 1972, p. 8.

the male readers in patriarchal Latin America who might feel redundant after reading this passage.

There are some male theologians, such as Enrique Dussel and Virgilio Elizondo,[6] who have seen connections between nationalist struggles and Marian devotion. Particularly in a continent such as Latin America, where Marian devotion has traditionally been more important than Christology, there have been links created among the poor and excluded and the figure of Mary. Some may argued that this has been done due to the fact that goddesses were worshipped under the guise of the Virgin Mary. In fact, some churches in Copacabana today show images of the Virgin Mary together with goddesses of Afro-Brazilian cults. However, the goddess connection may not be the only or most important reason for the popularity of the Marian worship among the poor. In fact the perceived marginality of Mary as a woman, and a vulnerable one at that, may have also played a role.

That the Virgin Mary image was used during wars of independence, for instance in Mexico, is a fact, although the details of the historical protagonists of such wars are more complex than theologians sometimes like to acknowledge. In fact, indigenous people thought that the Virgin Mary would help them to defeat the Spanish conquerors. Eventually they would leave Mexico and the indigenous nations would be free from the rule and religion of foreigners. Fighting against the Spanish under the banner of Mary might seem to indicate confused or contrary attitudes among those indigenous

---

6 See, for instance, Virgilio Elizondo's book on the Virgin of Guadalupe *La Morenita: Evangelizer of the Americas*, San Antonio, TX: Mexican American Cultural Centre Press, 1980. 'Morenita del Tepeyac' (lit. 'Dear Dark [Virgin] from the Tepeyac) is a title of the Virgin of Guadalupe. Enrique Dussel, a distinguished historian and philosopher of liberation from Argentin has done important research on the relationship between the worship of the Virgin of Guadalupe and the Mexican independence war. See E. Dussel (ed.) *La Iglesia en Latinoamérica 1492–1992*, New York: Orbis, 1992. Yet, from a Marxist thinker such as Dussel, one could have expected much more ideological criticism on the issue of the Guadalupean worship.

people. Nevertheless, in many countries the Virgin Mary has a long association with nationalism, for good or ill. Moreover, in this context it has been considered by some to be unpatriotic not to venerate Mary. Even feminist theologians are susceptible to accusations of not loving their nations, especially when their countries are suffering from economic and political oppression. That has not been an issue for Daly, but it has been an important one for Ivonne Gebara and Maria Clara Bingemer: they wrote a book dedicated to finding positive elements of action for poor women, but also for poor communities of men and women in Brazil.[7] What they did was a feminist Mariology of action which caught the imagination of many women living in poor conditions and provoked degrees of gender solidarity among men too. Mary had been interpreted from the perspective of elite men, and it was time that poor women could find another Mary, one who could identify with their struggles.

All these discussions and controversies have a common pattern: they are centred in Mariology from the perspective of gender roles. Mariology has been developed as a gendered Mariology, that is, highlighting negative gender prescriptions and finding subversive elements to help in deconstructing them. The deconstruction of a patriarchal Mary has been a project which has tried to illuminate gender patterns of thinking about Mary which needed to be challenged. Yet, in 2001 Althaus-Reid, an Argentinian theologian, adopted a different approach by reflecting on Mary within a sexual epistemological framework from a developing world perspective.[8] The attempt was to leave behind a more superficial discourse on gender in order to concentrate on sexuality. At this point the discussion surrounding Mary began to move beyond controversies of Mary the liberator versus Mary the passive woman, to become

---

7 The classic text on Mariology of liberation comes from Ivonne Gebara and Maria Clara Bingemer, *Mary: Mother of God, Mother of the Poor*, New York: Orbis, 1989.

8 Cf. Marcella Althaus-Reid, *Indecent Theology: Theological Perversions in Sex, Gender and Politics*, London: Routledge, 2001.

engaged in a different kind of discussion, in controversies within a queer/feminist frame of reference. There are different methodologies behind both positions and that fact is subsequently reflected in their Mariologies (or lack of them). The feminist Mariology may start with gender plus another relevant analysis, while the queer perspective concentrates on sexuality, not necessarily to attribute a certain sexuality to Mary, but to deconstruct her sexually. Mariology seems to have a close link with heterosexuality and has contributed somehow to the heterosexualization of Christian women. At the great ecclesial tea party men had by tradition organized the event, deciding who would make the tea, who would pour and who would receive it. When feminists came with their disruptive gender questions they insisted that they also could make and pour the tea. Queer theologians then came and uncovered the fact that feminists shared many assumptions with their male contenders about the essential rightness of things: Who decided we should all be drinking tea?

It is important at this point to emphasize that Mariology is not a central feminist theological project, and in fact only a minority of women concentrate on this theme. With the passage of time we cannot say that controversies surrounding the Virgin Mary remain as a decisive issue among feminist theologians. In fact, as the gender paradigm is displaced by a sexual paradigm it seems that the Virgin Mary thematic has lost its previous relevance. One can even argue that Mariology in feminist theology belongs to a previous era, related to the first wave of feminism which was obsessed with finding an equitable counterpart to the patriarchal system. Mary was seen as the feminine face of God. Her theological qualities became reversed: previously submissive she became courageous, previously passive now active. In general she was reconstructed to exhibit the virtues of the strong heroic women in the Bible. Yet, from the perspective of women who are not theologians but are devotees of the Virgin Mary, this has proved a mixed blessing. At various times it may well be that feminist Mariologies brought hope to many women experiencing oppression within their churches. But this comes at a price, for it has also perpetuated dependency on a patriarchal feminine symbol about whose subject little is known historically, but much has been constructed theologically. For Schüssler Fiorenza, in her book *Jesus: Miriam's Child, Sophia's Prophet* (1995) mainstream Mariology has had a negative effect on women on three accounts. First, the cult of virginity has been detrimental to women's sexuality. Second, it has paired together motherhood with the ideals of 'true womanhood'. And third, it has enforced values of passivity and submission upon women and gender relationships in general.[9] What she proposes is to find what she calls the subversive (or dangerous) side of Mary, not just by a different rereading of the scriptures but by a historical search to recover remembrances of Mary in ancient writings. For instance, there is the tradition that Mary was a young teenager raped by a Roman soldier. Only in this way, she claims, shall we be able to articulate a feminist discourse which not only affects Mariology, but also our understanding of Christ as the son of Mary. Moreover, Fiorenza advances the argument that Christian people should overcome their fear to the Goddess, a fear which she sees as has having been important for Israel's desire for a monopoly strategy of power (one God, one nation) but irrelevant for us today. There is no need to fear the Goddess elements that may be present in the popular worship of Mary).[10] Another first-wave feminist theologian, Rosemary Radford Ruether, has also attempted to overcome the stalemate in the now traditional debate of the Virgin Mary versus the Goddess. This she claims is a debate which is crucial, not because we need necessarily align ourselves with patriarchal Hebrew scriptures, but because it has become a crucible for the debate on female spirituality from the perspective of women. Therefore Ruether considers that Christianity needs to enter into a dialogue with the new pagan religiosity, although she deideologizes the goddess cults, which with few exceptions are seen by her as patriarchal

---

9 Elizabeth Schüssler Fiorenza, *Jesus: Miriam's Child, Sophia's Prophet: Critical Issues in Feminist Christologies*. London: Continuum, 1995, p. 164.

10 Schüssler Fiorenza, *Jesus: Miriam's Child, Sophia's Prophet*, p. 178.

constructs.[11] For Ruether, Mary is somehow the return of the Goddess and she wants to look at this beyond the wall dividing theologians. The way forward lies in a more ample perspective. In all this we are brought back to one of the key, core points of the Mariology controversies: Should Mariology be developed from women's experiences and should these also include female religious experiences from outside the patriarchal context of Judeo-Christianity?

However, the controversies surrounding Mary in feminist theology do not always link her with a spirituality which female authenticity derives from goddess cults. Latin American theologian Maria Clara Bingemer has, for instance, reworked a traditional position concerning the ordination of women in the Roman Catholic Church by doing a Mariology from the body. She declares that in Mary's body we have an example of the first Eucharist, because Jesus in her womb is part of a sacrament of a divine action of nourishing and sharing, symbolizing a feast of the ultimate liberation of humanity.[12] Mary could after all present a powerful argument not to disrupt, but to enlighten, our understanding of church hierarchies. A parallel line of argument to Bingemer's can be found in Tissa Balasuriya's controversial book *Mary and Human Liberation*.[13] Balasuriya's reflection, which led to his excommunication, considers the following points:

1 That Mary was born without sin, but that sin should not have any specific reference to sexuality and/or conception. By unveiling the pollution stigmas surrounding female sexuality in church traditions, Balasuriya goes as far as to say that everybody is born without sin, since human sexuality is not sinful as such.

---

11 See Rosemary Radford Ruether, *Goddesses and the Divine Feminine: A Western Religious History*, Berkeley: University of California Press, 2005, p. 301.

12 See Maria Clara Bingemer's article 'Women in the Future of Liberation Theology' in Marc Ellis and Otto Maduro (eds), *The Future of Liberation Theology: Essays in Honour of Gustavo Gutiérrez*, Orbis: 1989, p. 486.

13 Tissa Balasuriya, *Mary and Human Liberation: The Story and the Text*, London: Mowbray, 1997.

2   The construction of virginity in Mary needs to be acknowledged as dubious. There is no empirical knowledge to prove her subsequent virginity after the birth of Jesus.

3   The Mary of the Gospels (the historical Miriam) differs substantially from the Mary of theology, which has frequently been the product of controversial doctrines and power struggles of the church.

Balasuriya finds that there are no theological or biological grounds – and not certainly none around the symbolic figure of Mary – to deny women's ordination, and moreover, no reason why a woman could not become eventually a pope. Balasuriya, simply by reconstructing the Mary of the Gospels from the highly theologized Virgin Mary of the church traditions, has found that Mary is an important and liberative figure. It is obvious that Balasuriya is not a feminist theologian, but he is an Asian theologian who fully engaged for the purposes of researching his book with theologians such as Radford Ruether and Schüssler Fiorenza, as well as with liberation theologians such as Leonardo Boff. His book received the strong support of feminist theologians like Mary Grey who want to find the real Mary outside the misogynist traditions of the church. However, it is difficult to go back to the sources in order to produce a more authentic Mariology: the historical sources are almost non-existent. The Gospels say little and the church traditions are heavily patriarchalized. As Balasuriya suggests, his rereading of the Gospels seems the best option. Yet, for other feminist theologians, the Mary of the Gospels is not a figure to consider without taking into account her narrative contradictions. A text of liberation is counteracted with a declaration of female sexual submission. The empowered woman does not seem to have any political or religious consciousness and particularly she lacks what we today would call a feminist consciousness. Mary never discusses issues of female body pollution, or argues against discriminatory laws within Judaism. By comparison, other women in the Bible (probably more mature and experienced) had shown more feminist awareness, if the term can be used in such an anachronism. For instance, Judith prayed for women who have been raped and showed political and ecclesiastical shrewdness when dealing with serious difficulties in the life of her nation. Judith is presented in the Bible as an archetype and model for the Jewish woman of her time: intelligent, economically and emotionally independent, a good strategist and a courageous militant woman. By comparison, Mary, the mother of the Messiah, is a child, albeit a suffering one.

One of the most important works on a Mariology of liberation has been by Elina Vuola. She has done extensive research on this theme in Latin America, a continent which has been described with good reason as more Marian than Christian. For Vuola, Mariology is important in the context of Latin America for several reasons, mainly because she is the central figure of Christian worship in the continent, but also because she is the principal object of devotion among the poor, and specially, in the religiosity of poor women.[14] The fact that Mary has been constructed around the Original religions, including the Yoruba-based Umbanda and Santería cults, is not necessarily detrimental but speaks for the relevance given by the degree of inculturation of Marian worship among the poor. Moreover, for Vuola, Mariology is in general a good example of how sometimes theology is done 'from bottom to top' and not vice versa. Women's popular spirituality may have found a natural channel in the devotion to Mary. However, how would this explain the alienation produced by false gender consciousness regarding the worship of Mary in history?[15] In Latin America Mariology follows closely *marianismo*, that is, the construction of femininity based on the virtues of Mary, and the binary system of opposition between 'the virgin' and 'the whore' which permeates society with its dualism of *machismo–marianismo*. Here Vuola rejects a counterargument against the worship of Mary as the source for *marianismo*. For her,

14 Elina Vuola, 'Seriously Harmful for Your Health? Religion, Feminism and Sexuality in Latin America', in M. Althaus-Reid (ed.) *Liberation Theology and Sexuality*, London: Ashgate, 2006, pp. 137–62

15 Cf. Althaus-Reid, *Indecent Theology*, chapter 2 ('The Indecent Virgin').

this argument has been exaggerated and universalized, when in fact it may be representing only a middle-class ideal of femininity among certain Latin American elite groups. Moreover, she considers that popular Mariology, that is, the way that poor women represent the presence of Mary among them, and her leading role in the midst of their struggles, has influenced and subverted Mariology and not vice versa. Although Vuola is critical of the place of suffering as the ultimate metanarrative of poor Christian women and the role of Marian devotion in this, she also reflects on the fact that women do not necessarily accept the church's traditional Marian ideas of submission without negotiation. She finds that poor women in Latin America usually find through Mary a way to negotiate their everyday sufferings. They also find that their everyday lives and experiences, which the church never considered relevant, become through Mary 'divinized'. That is to say, ordinary women find a different relationship with the divine through Marian worship. However, these explanations do not seem to reflect enough on the fact that the Mariology is in itself, at least in Marian countries, a political institution. Mariology makes laws and sends women to jail, as in the recent example of Nicaragua when in 2006 nineteenth-century laws were revived to convict and punish with sentences of 30 years' imprisonment, male and female medical staff involved in performing therapeutic abortions.[16] A whole enforced consensus on sexual ethics, originating in a superstitious understanding of Mariology, has been crushing women (and men who are critical of patriarchalism) for centuries. Vuola's position comes from her own authentic theological work: she has done research with women's communities and reflects their struggles and theological negotiations. Yet, it could be argued that Mariology's sinister side lies not at the level of individual worship but at the level of institutions. How otherwise can we understand the fact that every dictatorial regime in Latin America has been strongly Marian? Or that authoritarianism and the worship

---

16 See 'Nicaragua Brings Abortion Laws' (Saturday, 18 November 2006). Available online, http://news.bbc.co.uk/2/hi/americas/6161396.stm

of Mary have been closely linked for centuries in the continent? To dismantle Mariology requires also a critical examination of the life of sociopolitical institutions. Mariology works as an ideology, illusive yet powerful and pervasive. It may not be possible to redeem it at a structural level. In fact, if we take the Roman Catholic Church as an example, we can see how historically Mary has never been represented as a metaphor for liberation. Why should it be different now?

Mariology is an area that highlights the contrast between the conception of femininity as maintained traditionally by the church and that of women living in the twenty-first century. In terms of using a hermeneutics of suspicion for Mariology based on class, race and culture, there are also different approaches. Black Madonnas have a powerful presence among some theologians, but once again it seems that the connection is made through another even more powerful goddess or symbolic earth-bonded female symbols. What we see in them is a projection from other symbolic religious systems, with different codes. We may well ask, Why worship a black virgin such as the Virgin of Copacabana instead of the Iemanjá (the Mother of the Sea in Afro-Brazilian religion)? It is evident that the Virgin Mary has been a lawful and permitted form which has given people the freedom to worship the Iemanjá. If that is the case, there is no Marian worship here, only a religious disguise found necessary in societies regulated by an authoritarian Roman Catholic Church. An authentic black Madonna would need to have not just a colour of skin, but a past, a culture and a history which may be incompatible with the Marian tradition.

Some women of the developing world have been keen to reflect on Mary from the perspective of her own vulnerability as a young, fragile, poor girl. Mary has been represented as a poor peasant girl, barefoot and simply dressed, carrying a baby in her arms: a sight all too common today in the slums and poor rural areas. There has been an attempt to produce an image involving class, not only considering Mary as a poor girl but especially including features that we today associate with marginality or destitution. For instance Mary has been identified with young and single mothers, or with mothers of political prisoners. In her vulnerability, it has been argued, lay her strength and every woman's strength. This is the position, for instance, of the Uruguayan theologian María Teresa Porcile Santiso mentioned at the outset, which eventually led her to understand the idea of God's own vulnerability.[17] Yet, no serious analysis of class and power relationships has ever been carried out on Mary. As tempting as it is to counterbalance patriarchal desires for power and control with Mary's own vulnerability, other theologians may consider that this image has the effect of justifying ecclesiastical arguments preventing women from attempting to claim power over their own lives. 'Fragility' is also part of a class-ridden argument: poor women do not have space in their lives to be fragile. Their struggle for life makes them in some senses stronger than women in many other communities. In any case, 'fragility' and 'vulnerability' are concepts which require analysis in order to mark the borders between victimization and patriarchal ideals of the woman as the perpetual, dependent child.

Politically, there is little we can say about Mary. Jesus and other characters from the biblical narratives do present in different ways criticism of the religious and political system of their time: Mary does not. Even to organize a Mariology within the framework of 'obedient girl/disobedient girl' requires a forced reading of the texts. In fact, the scriptural Mary never stands for other women's needs or rights. In the time of Jesus there were issues concerning pollution and the stoning or strangulation of women accused of adultery. Women's lives were severely regulated. Yet we are never told of any word or gesture of Mary which might lead us to believe that she had any consciousness – not of feminism (for that would be anachronistic) – but of solidarity with other women. It is no wonder that, as Vuola says, women in Latin America feel torn between being Christian or being feminists and asserting their rights.[18]

---

17 Cf. Maria Teresa Porcile Santiso, *La Mujer: Espacio de Salvación*, Perú: Trilce, 1991.

18 Cf. Vuola, 'Seriously Harmful for Your Health?', p. 161.

Mariology also requires a rereading of historic texts which might shed some light on the doctrinal rereadings which makes her trajectory in the life of the church so complex. For other theologians, Mary needs to be read in relationship with the Goddess movement, thealogy and women's spirituality outside the limitations of Christianity. At times, Mariology seems to be an empty symbol, which needs to be filled with extra meaningful material, as if Mary can no longer stand alone as a significant figure. There are major differences among feminist theologians precisely on the resources that they choose to use to make a case in favour of, or against, Mariology. As for the feminist theologians who are indifferent to Mary, that might in itself betray their negative feelings towards Mariology in general.

At the end of the day, Mariology confronts feminist theologians with many difficulties: the stereotyping of the feminine in Christianity but also perhaps in goddess cults, and the need to find authentic feminine symbols in the difficult patriarchal frame of Judeo-Christianity.

From here to queer; from Guadalupe to Ramona

Perhaps what can be said is that from Mary Daly's reflections on the Virgin Mary as the original rape of the Virgin and proceeding through Hampson's strong denial of the possibility of any feminine element which can be rescued from Mariology, feminist theologians have been able to consider and value the spiritual power of bargaining that women have in their everyday lives. This applies especially within poor communities where the need to find not just comfort but meaning and divine encouragement in the everyday struggle is strong. How then can feminist theologians claim that they do a theology which starts at the point of women stories and experiences, and yet deny women's positive, even liberative, relationships with the Virgin Mary? Yet what has to be taken into account is that women's experiences cannot simply be taken over without analysis. There are many elements of oppression in popular religiosity and ideological assumptions which require consideration. After all, as has been already noted, Mariology is not just a religious but a sociopolitical institution, at least in Marian countries. Unfortunately, liberation theologians tend to forget their structural analysis when it comes to women: historically issues relating to women have been dealt with in the private, domestic realm of individual experience. That was true of the powerful Mariology of race, culture and politics which was constructed around the figure of the Virgin of Guadalupe: her dark skin, her Maya eyes, her original native dress (lately slightly westernized) and the indigenous language she used when she addressed Juan Diego one night in the year 1533. Yet more was to come, as the Guadalupana became a political, mystical leader of the war of independence in Mexico: now as then, a powerful nationalist symbol.

As the twenty-first century begins, we might wonder if even the best Mariology of Liberation such as the Guadalupana will still be relevant in a century when feminist theology has been found somewhat struggling between more radical gender and sexuality paradigms, and more hermeneutical suspicions. Mary's sexuality and political identity seem more important than before, but Mary is a theological device which eludes sexuality and politics. Yet in queer theologies women do not look necessarily for women role models or female spirituality in the Bible, at least not in the same way as before. Queer, transgressive women may identify with queer transgressive men, and vice versa. The identification of women with other women obeys different paradigms of radical stance and transgressiveness. Mary's positive role, as for instance the Virgin of Guadalupe, may be theologically diminished. Even the Virgin Mary of the communities of poor women may be changing rapidly: the Zapatistas portrayal of the Virgin Mary as a guerrilla woman, carrying a child on her hip and a gun at her waist. The Philippine Mary is the mother of a revolutionary. The queer Mary is a transvestite, dancing in the streets of Sao Paulo, while singing political carnival songs. There is also the famous painting, the 'Virgin of Dietrich' displayed in a gay pub in Rio de Janeiro, which portrays Marlene Dietrich as the Dolorosa. As an example of how the Virgin of Guadalupe has been superseded in postmodern Latin America, the well-known Comandante Ramona, who died in January 2006, has been identified by Maya Tzotzil and Tzeltal indigenous women as their personification of the Virgin Mary. A common phrase supporting this says that she was *una mujer de mucha enagua* ('a woman of many petticoats') signifying her strength but also her sexuality. Curiously, Ramona never wanted her biography to be known: as with the Virgin Mary, it starts with the moment of conversion to a noble cause. Somehow there is no fragility or vulnerability here, but unusually for a Latin American woman, she is a woman without a past which can silence or condemn her. However, this is a reversed Mariology: here Mary is constructed from the image of Ramona, and not vice versa. Ramona never spoke Spanish, only Tzotzil and other Mayan languages, but she was the leader who took a town, San Cristóbal de las Casas, to protest against the North American trade agreement.[19]

It could be that we are starting to find that Mariology needs to depart from Mary, and that perhaps it has always been so. However, the different arguments and controversies surrounding Marian worship among feminist theologians show that we are rapidly moving beyond the original disagreements concerning for instance her passivity, or the biological impossibilities of her condition of virgin and mother. These issues have been a source of alienation for so many generations, including their contribution to crimes arising from the overcommodification of virginity for women. It seems that popular Mariologies are formed by reversal (as in the case of Ramona), but also are queer Mariologies, less preoccupied with biological definitions of who is who in the Bible. Even the case for Mary Magdalene, who has become popular as the counterradical figure to Mary, is still at least in popular circles, heavily heterosexual, and used to ensure that Jesus is constructed as a heterosexual. Gender

---

19 Cf. Phil Davison, 'Obituary: Comandante Ramona' (9 January 2006), available online http://news.independent.co.uk/people/obituaries/article337439. ece

and sexual paradigms create serious differences for Mariologies. They not only pose different questions, but also have stronger sociopolitical implications which require a different style of theological reflection. Mary as Ramona leads her people in the struggle of life; Mary in the Gospels tried to persuade Jesus to return home to Nazareth.

4

Christology

Feminist Christology has moved a long way since the early days of questioning whether a male saviour could in fact save women. That question in itself appeared to imply that the saving nature of Jesus was beyond investigation and that what would be shifted through the examination would be the patriarchal overlay of an otherwise sound doctrine. As we see much more than that moved and remains moving once women turn their attention and lived experience to the nature and significance of the person, Jesus. Indeed so much has been written in this area that it is not possible to do justice to it all. Therefore, the questions considered will be representative of a larger debate.

The crux of the original question about the male saviour and women remains relevant today when we see time and again restatements of a Christ through church decrees that speak very little to women. The western feminist line of thinking on this is that the figure of Christ has been so constructed by patriarchal thinking, as have women, that one gets left out of any reflection on the nature of the other. Rosemary Radford Ruether was one of the first feminist thinkers to examine where the denial of the female first infiltrated a religion that declared a new social order. She finds the origin of the denial of the feminine in the classical Neo-Platonism and apocalyptic Judaism out of which Christianity was born. Here we find the combination of a male warrior God with the exaltation of the intellect over the body. The alienation of the masculine from the feminine is the basic sexual symbol that sums up all the other dualisms which are mind and body; subjective self and objective world; individual and community; autonomous will (male) and bodily sensuality (female); and the domination of nature by spirit.[1] In addition the Hellenistic influence has shaped concepts such as Logos and Christ in devastatingly androcentric ways.[2] While Christianity has never claimed that God was literally male, the Hellenistic underpinning has led to many assumptions about the nature of God and therefore what constitutes normative humanity. There has been an unspoken, yet enacted, androcentric bias, which has reduced the place of women and men in the world holding them as it does to very outmoded and reductive notions of humanness. Within this scenario women have lost out much more than men who can at least, as Mary Daly reminds us, claim that God is male and therefore they are made in a special image! By simply refusing to believe the rhetoric of the innate inferiority of women, feminist theologians are bringing into question the entire androcentric/patriarchal logic that has to date underpinned christological debates. They are in a very profound way questioning the ability of a male saviour to save women.

Interestingly those who we in the West may view as particularly oppressed by the androcentric nature of Christology do not always have the same problems as we do with the maleness of Christ. Indeed, in certain cultures it is a positive advantage that Jesus, a man, could concern himself with women at all. For example, Filipino women do not find the maleness of Jesus to be a problem in their Christology. Indeed, born, as he was, a male, they believe he was in the best position to challenge the male definition of humanity and male privilege that is built on that definition. In addition, it is his power as a male within society that enables him to offer a more affective challenge to men to change their ways in the here and now.

---

1 Rosemary Ruether, 'Motherearth and the Megamachine: A Theology of Liberation in a Feminine, Somatic and Ecological Perspective', in C. Christ and J. Plaskow (eds), *Womanspirit Rising: A Feminist Reader on Religion*, San Francisco: Harper and Row, 1979, p. 44.

2 Rosemary Ruether, *Introducing Redemption in Christian Feminism*, Sheffield: Sheffield Academic Press, 1998, p. 82.

Monica Melancton demonstrates how some Indian theologians deal with the problems of the maleness and male identification of Jesus. This she says is part of the historical Jesus but it does not mean that it is an essential ingredient of the risen Christ who is dwelling in the redeemed order.[3] This risen Christ transcends all particularities. In this way the maleness of Jesus can no longer dictate the femaleness of all women through time, he becomes the symbol of a new humanity rather than a model of gender enactments.

Indian women's Christology emphasizes that Jesus was a saviour for women within their own patriarchal situation. He did not judge them by the standards that their society set, for example, he did not condemn the adulteress nor did he shun the Samaritan woman who had many husbands. He healed them, even when their illnesses would have made him unclean in the eyes of his society. Also, and crucially, he did not exclude them from what might be seen as the 'deeper things', for example, his teaching and the revelation of his being. The women around Jesus, it is argued, actually understood his significance more easily than the male disciples and tended to his needs more than his male colleagues were able to. They remained faithful when others fled. Jesus reached out to women and they to him in a mutual embrace of recognition and respect. It is this Christ who they hope will stem the tide of dowry brides, temple prostitution and widow burning. Indian Christian women place their hope in the woman-loving Christ to raise the literacy level among women and to gain more stable employment rights for women. They also hope that rape and physical abuse both inside and outside the family will decrease. Of course, Christ will not do this through magic but through the realization that Jesus thought women were human too and deserved the dignity and celebration attached to all God's creation. It is the Christ who as a male, acted against 'male culture' who gives hope to many women in India. The message of women's

---

3 Monica Melancton, 'Christology and Women', in Virginia Fabella and Sun Ai Lee Park, *We Dare to Dream: Doing Theology as Asian Women*, Hong Kong: AWCCT, 1989, p. 18.

dignity is, within that culture, more powerfully heard when spoken by a man. Jesus is the male advocate par excellence and his gender is less of a problem than his colonial crown.[4]

For many feminist theologians the 'scandal of particularity' is no scandal at all. That Jesus was a first-century male son of a carpenter and the son of the eternal God sits easily with some. As we see with the work of theologians from the Philippines and India the 'problems' are thought to be overcome by the assertion that Jesus was a man quite unlike others of his time and culture, that is he embraced women and included them in his message. Ruether is not happy with this solution since she believes we do have to admit the particularity of Jesus and deal with it in a mature way. She reminds us that classical Christology has prided itself on the dissolution of all particularity and look where that has got us. She says:

> I believe we should encounter Jesus, not only as male, but in all his particularity as a first century Galilean Jew. We then must ask how we can see him as paradigmatic of universal human redemption in a way that can apply to female as well as male, to people of all ethnicities and cultures.[5]

Here Ruether frees us from biological determinism and spiritual infancy in one majestic move. By prioritizing the message and not the gender Christians become 'redemptive community not by passively receiving a redemption "won" by Christ alone, but rather by collectively embodying this path of liberation in a way that transforms people and social systems'.[6] The Christ who is to come is then understood to be 'the fullness of all this human diversity gathered together in redemptive community'.[7] This understanding of Christology does away with patriarchal order and integrates an equalitarian

---

4 For more on the colonial Christ, see Lisa Isherwood, *Liberating Christ*, Cleveland, OH: Pilgrim Press, 1999.

5 Ruether, *Introducing Redemption*, p. 93.

6 Ruether, *Introducing Redemption*, p. 93.

7 Ruether, *Introducing Redemption*, p. 94.

understanding of human nature into Christology. But the question remains and the controversy rages over whether this is another dominant cultural export.

So even before we have begun to consider matters of doctrine to do with Christology, we have met an area where opinions differ and the lived experience of one group of women is distinct from that of another. This is the great strength of feminist theologies, that difference does not mean division. The reason for this may well lie in the fact that Christology for feminist theology is largely an ethical affair and so if the models fit the continued empowerment and liberation of women they can be understood by those who would not in their own lives find the same models so empowering. There are, however, I believe edges to this accepting utopian sisterhood as I think we will see!

If for the moment we turn our attention to a central concept in patriarchal Christology, that of the Suffering Servant, we again have illustrated the difference in opinion that emerges within feminist theologies. The image of a son sacrificed to his father in order that good may come of it is a common theme in masculinist mythology since these stories tend to establish a bond between the father and son and are the glue of male bonding and the passing on of culture; fathers teaching son's lessons about the role of the hero and the glory of sacrifice. Not unsurprisingly women have struggled in this world of male bonding and have found themselves to be alienated by the story or victimized by it. Women have found that their lives do not speak of sacrifice and suffering as salvific but rather that it is crushing of the very humanity they strive to rejoice in. Womanist theologians were among the first to engage critically with the notion of glorious sacrifice. Coming as they do from a situation where slavery is a recent memory they were suspicious of doctrine that appeared to justify suffering and death. Delores Williams[8] is adamant that the cross legitimizes the surrogacy experience of black women; it makes

---

8 Delores Williams, *Sisters in the Wilderness: The Challenge of Womanist God-Talk*, New York: Orbis, 1993.

the bearing of other people's burdens legitimate when in fact it is inhumane. She says:

> The cross is a reminder of how humans have tried throughout history to destroy visions of right relationships that involve transformation of tradition and transformation of social relations and arrangements sanctioned by the status quo.[9]

As Christians black women cannot forget the cross but they would be unwise to glorify it as this could make their exploitation sacred. What is true in the USA is also true in many parts of Africa where women are cautious about the idealization of suffering on a continent that is bleeding to death. It may seem that they would, in the face of the devastation of AIDS and the apparent inability to do anything to stop it, take some comfort in the idea of glory associated with uncalled for suffering, but they do not.

The doctrine of the sacrifice and death of Jesus has been a tricky one for womanists who on the face of it wish to reject it outright as part of a crippling heritage. However, if they are careful with their history they have to admit that many of their foremothers found great comfort in the idea that Jesus could save them from their suffering through his own. That he could understand what it was like to feel the lash and to be abused meant for many that the deep connection they could forge with him was their only strength in a world that otherwise alienated them. As the spirituals remind us there is a strong strand of theology formed in slavery that considered only Jesus, and not God, could feel the oppression and so bring hope.

The problems of Suffering Servant models of Christ go beyond that of the womanist community and impact on the lives of millions of women worldwide through the increasing reality of domestic

---

9 Delores Williams, 'Black Women's Surrogate Experience and the Christian Notion of Redemption', in *After Patriarchy: Feminist Transformations of the World Religions*, William Eakin, Jay B. McDaniel and Paula Cooey (eds), New York: Orbis, 1991, p. 12.

violence. There are many reasons for domestic abuse[10] and of course Christianity is not to blame for all of them. However, Christians need to take note of the high levels within traditional Christian homes and to ask whether there is some excuse for this lurking in their doctrinal systems. Traditional theologies of the cross present us with a model of divine child abuse and strong obedience and dependency models. These models are not helpful to women in an androcentric world. The supreme example of the suffering of Christ has held many women in abusive situations and has numbed the pastoral response of many clerics. Christine Gudorf has demonstrated how the sacrifice of surrogate victims does not interrupt the violence but rather rechannels it because the perpetrator is protected from the protests of the victim and any consequences for his actions.[11] By ritualizing the suffering and death of Jesus into a salvific act Christian theology has disempowered the oppressed and abused and therefore encouraged the cycle of abuse. It appears that while we continue to think of the death of Jesus as salvific by its very nature, instead of an outrageous act of public torture and social control, we put the lives of women at risk.

As we have come to expect the picture of even the Suffering Servant differs with each context. In Korea some of the feminist work is based in a female identification of Jesus which is carried through the connections made between him and Kuan Yin. Kuan Yin is the compassionate goddess of the common-folk who symbolizes relatedness, community and suffering. She is a celestial bodhisattva who hears the cries of the world.[12] She is also a personification of wisdom and appears to people who are in need. Her suffering is connected with her wisdom and is seen as redemptive but in a radically different

---

10 The latest government report shows that an incident of domestic violence occurs every 17 seconds in the United Kingdom.

11 Christine Gudorf, quoted in Elisabeth Schüssler Fiorenza and Shawn Copeland, *Violence Against Women*, London: Concilium, 1994, p. 14.

12 Naomi F. Southard, 'Recovery and Rediscovered Images: Spiritual Resources for Asian American Women', in Ursula King, *Feminist Theology from the Third World*, London: SPCK, 1994, p. 383.

way from that of Jesus. Kuan Yin is a wise sufferer, that is, she may walk a painful path but in so doing she sees the radical possibilities for change. This is a powerful message for women who often suffer for no good reason and have not believed that transformation should be the goal of their suffering. Korean women get a better perspective on their own suffering through the combination of their own culture with that of Christianity; they become able to see their own position as that of transformative, redemptive suffering. The Korean imaging of Christ from below means that a hero or a mighty ruler would be an inappropriate understanding of the one who would be called saviour in the Korean context. Christ does not arrive triumphant in the lives of the oppressed but rather,

> emerges from the broken-body experience of workers when they affirm life and dare to love other human beings in spite of their brokenness. Workers become Christ to each other when they touch each other's wounds and heal each other through sharing food, work and hope.[13]

The sharing of these resources, particularly food, is another way in which the Suffering Servant is understood, he is in the face of suffering, the communal will to live. This is a rather different view from that held in the West.

However, many Korean women do start, as do some womanists, with Jesus as their co-sufferer. Imaged as the Suffering Servant they believe he is able to know their true feelings and empathize with them. This model shouts loudly that domination is never right and it is this message that the women need to hear. They are also able to find meaning in their own suffering, not in the traditional way of supposing it will bring them rewards in heaven, but by viewing it as redemptive for others, just as Jesus' suffering was said to be. Chung Hyun Kyung is aware of the particular dangers for Korean women, they have had a very mixed message about suffering both from their

---

13 Chung Hyun Kyung, *Struggle to Be the Sun Again: Introducing Asian Women's Theology*, London: SCM Press, 1990, p. 7.

own culture and from the colonizers. She fears that some may find it easier to accept the Suffering Servant role in the traditional sense as this is all they have ever known. They are encouraged to love Jesus and to suffer while he seems largely absent from their lives. Chung asks if this is the only model they know as it is reminiscent of their fathers, husbands and lovers.[14] However, it does seem to be the case that the Suffering Servant model of Jesus can afford many a sense of self-worth and dignity since he went through what they experience and he came out with dignity. It is this dignity that provides hope for the future and enables them to believe they are engaged in redemptive praxis for themselves and others.

Of course the whole question of redemption has also come under the feminist gaze and many ask, along with Daly, whether sin and salvation are myths springing from male arrogance. So is there anything for a saviour to save us from? We are all familiar with the work of feminist theologians who have very convincingly argued against the received wisdom of the Fall and therefore against the need to be redeemed from it, but where does this leave a central concept in Christology? Mary Grey argues from a relational view of Christ that is held by many feminist theologians and says,

> If the relational process is at the heart of the reality of the great divine creative–redemptive dynamism, participating in this must be what is meant by holiness. So entering into deeper more meaningful and at the same time juster structures of relating is the kind of redemptive spirituality needed for the transformation of the world. Sin must therefore be acting against the relational grain of living.[15]

Grey is adamant that creation and redemption are linked and in the light of current ecological destruction we would be unwise to move away entirely from notions of redemption. It could be argued that

---

14 Chung, *Struggle to Be the Sun Again*, p. 54.

15 Mary Grey, *Redeeming the Dream: Feminism, Redemption and Christian Tradition*, London: SPCK, 1989, p. 35.

these deeply embedded religious motifs can still provide a way of standing outside the current crisis and envisaging a new way, a redemptive way, for the earth and its inhabitants. For Grey women also need the redemptive process of self-affirmation. For Grey self-affirmation and right relation go hand in hand, since without an affirmation of self we are not in a position to enter and negotiate right, just and mutual relation. Therefore, Grey continues to argue that salvation/redemption are not outmoded concepts but are as necessary today as at the time of Jesus. Salvation, of course, is not dispensed from the great God/hero but is rather painfully striven for in the global community among justice-seekers.

Among those who reject the idea of the redeeming saviour role for Christ it is not surprising to find great emphasis on the liberating power of Christ which is rooted in social and economic justice. In the West Rosemary Ruether was among those who declared that Christ was best understood as a liberator, not in the spiritual sense, but in real terms in the political and social realm. Ruether wished to take seriously the Jewish roots of Christianity and Christian thinking and so was not prepared to merely brush over Hebraic messianic thought with the gloss of Greek metaphysics. Central to Jewish messianic hope was political action, since for the Jews religious and political life were synonymous. Even when their ideas around the kingdom became more transcendent they never lost sight of the importance of politics. In fact they got thrown into sharp relief and adopted a more radical edge. The Messiah was always understood as a political figure who would champion the poor and the oppressed, he would be a king of Israel. Ruether thinks there is enough in the tradition that can be liberated to turn patriarchal interpretations on their heads. She views the task as that of struggling with Jesus for the transformation of the world, beginning with an option for the poor and oppressed. For her Christology does a number of things apart from calling us to seek justice. It also makes us recognize the interconnected nature of injustice and to admit to the role of dominant ideologies in the perpetuation of injustices. Most importantly, of course, we have to admit that the fullness of the

Christ event is connected with the coming of the kingdom. The latter is plainly not here and so Christology has a 'partial' feel, that is those qualities we call Christlike in the life of Jesus are still to come to fullness. The expected Messiah has not come and to pretend that he has simply helps us to be numbed to injustice and suffering in the here and now. Ruether claims that Jesus can act as a sign of messianic blessedness to those who wish to see him that way, but rightly understood he is one among many who signal that another order is possible, that which we call the kingdom of God. Ruether challenges Christianity to see the events of Jesus' life as eschatological, as realities towards which we are still moving, and not as historical events that form the base of an established church. The kingdom is not here even though there are moments when the transcendent becomes present in an anticipatory way through justice, liberation and reconciliation. These moments are never more than relative and indeed should not be made absolute. For Ruether, Jesus is not yet the Christ but is a paradigm for hoping and aspiring; Christ is the fulfilment of that hope.

Rita Brock is critical of Ruether claiming that she places Jesus in the position of a hero, despite the unfinished nature of his role, and thus disables his followers. We give away our own power to those we consider heroes, and this is made no better by the fact that we view the hero as benevolent or even the Christ, we are still left bereft of control in our lives. She is adamant that basing Christology on a historical figure is a mistake since it confuses the concept with the phenomenon.[16] We should be placing the saving events of Christianity in a much broader context than that of the person of Jesus. She understands the shift in feminist Christology to be from seeing Jesus as the focus of redemption to seeing him as the locus of faith. To illustrate her point she looks at the miracle stories which she does not wish to explain away, but rather to claim them as normative statements about the nature of Christian community. They show

---

16 See Rita Brock, *Journeys by Heart: A Christology of Erotic Power*, New York: Crossroad, 1988.

clearly what is possible when we are functioning from the level of connection and not operating with a power-over model. In other words they illustrate the liberating power of Christ in relation and the political nature of illness. Healing, then, is not something bestowed by one with power but is striven for by the whole community in a relationship of power equality.

Mary Grey also fires a warning to Ruether against viewing redemption as simply justice: 'Redemption seeks to transform the world at a deeper level than do the movements for freedom and liberation – yet it must include them'.[17] Redemption carries with it more than social implications, although these will manifest. Our passion for justice increases our participation in the divine creative ground of our existence. As we become more like God so God will become more tangible in the world as the one who unites feeling, energy and action. While involved in our own self-awakening and development we are also in relation to a profounder process, a cosmic energy that enables us to develop our own visionary powers, which are beyond gender. For Grey Jesus shows how growth in connection can present a radical challenge and lead to transformative action. She illustrates that this was an understanding that Jesus himself had to move towards and she suggests that he had three distinctive periods in his own understanding of salvation, which at its deepest level was much more than that of the radical freedom fighter, although it began there.[18]

For theologians such as Carter Heyward the whole christological project actually begins with the man Jesus and not some abstract Logos. Heyward believes it is a crippling mistake to see Jesus as a divine person rather than as a human being who knew and loved God. It is crippling because it prevents people claiming their own divinity. She does not deny the possibility of incarnation, indeed if God is a God of relation then incarnation is bound to be not only a possibility but a desirable necessity. She is not devaluing the reality of incarnation but rather exposes the limits of exclusivity.

17 Grey, *Redeeming the Dream*, p. 87.
18 Grey, *Redeeming the Dream*, p. 96.

Heyward does not wish to deny God's parenthood of Jesus but wishes to reimage beyond genetic terms and therefore as the source of power in which Jesus was grounded. Once we really value Jesus' humanity the dualistic gulf between humanity and God is breached. It becomes possible to assert that our own humanity can touch, heal and comfort the world and in so doing strengthen God. At the same time it becomes apparent that a God of love is as dependent on us as we are on her.

Heyward therefore reimages divinity as something we grow towards by choice and activity. This shift requires her to look critically at the notions of authority and power. She is anxious to move away from the idea that authority is something that is exercised over us by God or state and to come to an understanding of it as self-possessed. Heyward notes that two words are used in the Gospels. One is *exousia*, which denotes power that has been granted, in contrast to *dunamis*, which is raw power – innate, spontaneous and often fearful – not granted but inborn. This latter is the authority that Jesus claims. What was new about Jesus, Heyward claims, was his realization that our *dunamis* is rooted in God and is the force by which we claim our divinity. When humans dare to acknowledge their divine nature through *dunamis*, this is the kind of kingdom that is imaginable and must be made incarnate through radical love. Radical love incarnates the kingdom because intimacy is the deepest quality of relation. Heyward says that to be intimate is to be assured that we are known in such a way that the mutuality of our relation is real, creative and cooperative. It is possible to see Jesus' ministry as based on intimacy since he knew people intuitively, insightfully and spontaneously.

Heyward's Christ is one who meets us where we are between the 'yet' and the 'not yet' and impresses upon us not so much the nature of the Christ but the meaning of who we are.[19] Therefore the Christ

---

19 Carter Heyward, *The Redemption of God*, Lanham: University of America Press, 1982, p. 163.

is a friend who empowers not a God who will manipulate. In this way, 'God's incarnations are as many and varied as the persons who are driven by the power in relation to touch and be touched by sisters and brothers.'[20] Most of all, Heyward's Christology is fully embodied, sensuous and erotic, seeking vulnerable commitment, alive with expectancy and power. Heyward is only too well aware that traditional Christianity will have difficulty accepting such an experientially based Christology, based as it is in lesbian embodiment.

She was not of course wrong, indeed many feminist theologians from around the world expressed concern over the emphasis on the erotic element of Christology. It seems that at times they did not fully understand that Heyward was understanding erotic in a much wider sphere than the purely sexual and through this narrow understanding they were uneasy. It seemed to many that women were once again being understood as the fleshy and sexual side of human nature, which is how we were seen in much traditional Christology, rather than being released in a wider appreciation of who we are. To others, particularly those from places such as Thailand and the Philippines, it seemed that a sexual emphasis in relation to our godding was missing the point and the reality of the far-ranging sexual exploitation of women. In short, it was another western construct that completely overlooked the reality of many women. All of this was, of course, before the concerns over a particularly lesbian approach were even considered. While most understand that Heyward speaks from her experience and that has a real place in feminist theology, there are those who regret that her Christology of relationality has been spoken of as most effective and achievable between women. In truth this statement by her was a reflection rather than a defining moment and perhaps not too much should be made of it, but it does highlight the fact that divisions between women's experience do exist and will have christological consequences.

---

20 Heyward, *The Redemption of God*, p. 164.

Marcella Althaus-Reid welcomes the way in which the Christ-ology of Heyward and others has allowed us to look again at what she sees as romanticized christological images. In her eyes we have not looked closely enough at what the erotic nature of Christology might actually mean and she welcomes the chance to do so. In libera-tion theology we sit easy with the Christ who embraces the poor and such images as Christ the Peruvian peasant on the cross symbolize this for us in a convincing but ultimately not very challenging way. For Althaus-Reid this is not even half the story as it does not shift the christological core far enough, it does not embrace the reality of lived experience and poverty in a brutal enough way. If the truly poor are to be embraced then we should be imaging Christ as a young girl prostituted by two men in a public toilet in Buenos Aires.[21] Althaus-Reid argues that a failure in all liberation theology has been that it has fought for equality but not for diversity, therefore the reality of very many women's lives has been left out of the process of christological reflection. She argues that a new understanding of Christ is needed – one that moves away from Christ as the fetish of Christianity and the patriarchal discourse that underpins it. She argues that by telling the sexual stories that are the reality of real people's lives, we destabilize normative rules which cripple people, and that this is a Christic act.

Althaus-Reid offers many challenging images of Christ, among them Christ as Xena, warrior princess; a leather clad woman hang-ing on a cross, declaring love unto eternity for the woman she loves. She is not passive, she is in leather and she is a dyke. She is coura-geous and transgressive just as Jesus of Nazareth was and so we are faced with the question, is she a Christ? Certainly she is because she destabilizes the neat patriarchal hierarchy, which rests on Christ the celibate heterosexual. She is the sort of Christ that women need, one who will free them from preconceptions and deathly stereotypes.

Many of us are now very comfortable with images of a female

---

21 Marcella Althaus-Reid, *Indecent Theology: Theological Perversions in Sex, Gender and Politics*, London: Routledge, 2001.

Christ, so much so that it is not too exaggerated to say that she does have a place in some mainstream theology and religious imagining. However, the edges of this comfort are met and challenged for many with the introduction of such female images as Xena warrior Christ, or the child prostitute Christ spoken of by Althaus-Reid.[22] After all the young girl being prostituted in a public toilet does represent the most marginalized and the poorest of the poor in the Argentinean context, and many more besides. So why should we hide our faces from this grim reality when we are happy to talk about Christ of the poor? Despite questioning why we do this, it still seems to be true that these images are a step too far for many Christians, almost an insult to the Christ we are attempting to speak about. It has puzzled me for some time as to why this should be, after all we have moved a long way in feminist theology, and in terms of Christology we do broadly accept that whatever the Christ may be it is an outworking among us in the intimate concerns of our lives. Why then should we draw a line in the sand and find some parts of life unacceptable areas for reflection on the divine? Surely if we are declaring incarnation to be a more all-encompassing event than the one pure Son of God, then nothing can be beyond reflection?

I think that despite the huge advances in feminist theologies the lines are still drawn around the body, that is to say when the body gets too vocal in the creation of Christology it has to be silenced since it still sits under the influence of dualistic metaphysics. Despite the moves in feminist theology to eradicate that insidious mindset, I feel that the lines we draw are affected by the sense that some bodies and experiences are just not good enough – how could we have this view unless we have a notion of what is good enough and where do we, as Christians, find that sense? When we read the Gospels we do not get a sense of the narrow confines of those who are acceptable to the man Jesus and so it must come from somewhere else. I have argued many times that the 'somewhere else' is Greek metaphysics that infected and altered a radical theology based in the lived experi-

---

22 See Althaus-Reid, *Indecent Theology*, passim.

ence of women and men into a constricting set of codes governed by Platonic absolutes. It seems that as far as we have come we have further to go and this is in the direction of challenging not just dualism but metaphysics themselves. We need to ask the question whether we can have a non-metaphysical Christ. I have argued elsewhere[23] that we can, and further that in so doing we gift ourselves the full potential of incarnation – we invite ourselves to enter our human–divine natures more fully and in so doing to make countercultural living a reality, embodying the kingdom on earth.

It is also my contention that in understanding our Christology without the hindering veil of metaphysics, we are actually closer to the intention of Jesus than we have previously been. I am in line with Heyward's Christology but go a little further – I believe that where we differ is in my insistence on the immanent nature of the divine whereas for Heyward there remains an element that is removed and beyond us. I wish to be clear that I do experience and understand that the whole is greater than the sum of the parts, that is to say at times we appear to be in the presence of something much bigger than ourselves. This I understand as the communal nature of Christ that becomes manifest when those who are in relationality and attempting to find mutual empowerment are working together, being silent together or reflecting together. I do not understand this as springing from beyond us but rather feel it as the generous outpouring of incarnation which was signalled by the man Jesus as the birthright of all. These moments are the breaking through of the challenge to embody the Christ we proclaim we believe in. As might be expected this view will not be met with full agreement by all feminist theologians who still wish to maintain something metaphysical in the nature of Christ. I continue to maintain that the story of incarnation as told in the Gospels has not been tried because of this metaphysical veil, a veil that had no place in the kind of Judaism that seems to be espoused by the early Jesus movement. I suggest

---

23 Lisa Isherwood, 'Jesus Past the Posts', in Lisa Isherwood and Kath McPhillips, *Post Christian Feminisms*, London: Ashgate, 2007.

that once we remember that Judaism at the time of Jesus had many faces and that he and his followers had a rich and diverse tradition from which to draw and on which to build, we can look again and question strongly the notion that dualism and metaphysics had to be part of their own understanding. One step along this path is aided by Sophiaology.

Elisabeth Schüssler Fiorenza[24] claims that Jesus was in the Sophia tradition of Judaism and that this can be demonstrated from scripture. The Hebrew scriptures of course talk about Sophia and it is here that she is most visible. However, the Christian scriptures, particularly the Johannine literature, highlight a stage when Jesus is given the attributes of Sophia. It is Schüssler Fiorenza's claim that some of the earliest traditions of the Jesus movement understood Jesus as the prophet of Sophia who was to make the realm of God available to the poor and marginalized. As a child of Sophia he also made the message experientially available to all through ministry and miracles. One of the earliest Jesus sayings states that 'Sophia is justified by her children' (QLK 7.35) which signifies that Sophia is with all her children and is made just in and by them. The statements that have been hijacked to proclaim Jesus' atoning death can be seen in a different light as confirming that Jesus was the prophet of Sophia, for example, 'Therefore also the Wisdom of God said, "I will send them prophets and apostles, some of whom they will kill and persecute"' (Luke 13.34). This suggests that the earliest reflections on the nature of Jesus were sophialogy not Christology. Fiorenza wants to argue that Jesus does not close the Sophia tradition by being the last and greatest,[25] as this would be the contradiction of the tradition, rather he opens it yet further and invites us all to join. He stands in a long line of Sophia prophets both men and women who have been killed for the message they bring. Their deaths were not willed by Sophia, indeed they are lamented (QLK

24 Elisabeth Schüssler Fiorenza, *Jesus: Miriam's Son, Sophia's Prophet: Critical Issues in Feminist Christologies*, New York: Continuum, 1995.

25 Schüssler Fiorenza, *Jesus: Miriam's Son*, p. 8.

13.34). Thus sophialogy helps overcome the anti-Jewish tendencies inherent in traditional Christology, which as we shall see in a moment still haunt even feminist Christology.

Many scholars think that Jesus replaced Sophia, but according to Fiorenza close examination of the texts shows that Jesus is handed the attributes that Sophia always possessed (Matt. 11.25-7), receiving them from her.[26] The Father God does give Jesus knowledge but Sophia, who was present at creation with YHWH, already has the qualities that Jesus inherits from the Father. Fiorenza explains the exclusive father/son language as the drawing of boundaries by the early communities. The baptism of Jesus confirms the view that he was a prophet of Sophia as she descended upon him like a dove (the grey dove was the symbol of the immanent Sophia while a turtle dove was a symbol of her transcendence). Further, just like Sophia Jesus found no dwelling place among humans and so was given one in heaven (Enoch 42.1-2; Sir. 24.3-7). Similarly they were both exalted and enthroned assuming rulership over the whole cosmos (Phil. 2.6-11; Isa. 45.23). The latter echoes the Isis cult and so it is no surprise that Jesus too is called Lord which was the title given to Isis. The Christ is understood in terms of Sophia as the mediator of the first creation and as the power of a new qualitatively different creation. It is this understanding of Sophia that allowed Christianity to have a cosmic agenda, to believe it could change the world.

Elisabeth Johnson[27] is another scholar who wishes to develop the notion of Jesus as that of Jesus-Sophia. She is convinced that the early church used many of the traditions about personified Wisdom in order to come to an understanding of who Jesus was. Indeed, she asserts that it was only after he had become identified with wisdom that he was understood as the only-begotten son. This signals a

---

26 Schüssler Fiorenza, *Jesus: Miriam's Son*, p. 30

27 Elisabeth Johnson, 'Redeeming the Name of Christ', in *Freeing Theology: The Essentials of Theology in Feminist Perspective*, Catherine Mowry LaCugna (ed.), New York: Harper, 1993.

slight difference between the theories of Schüssler Fiorenza and Johnson. Schüssler Fiorenza, as we have seen, has no desire to view all the attributes of Jesus as the last word, indeed she wishes to see the fact that he could live as he did as an invitation to us all to do the same – his life and way of living is an invitation we can all accept and further achieve. This may not be the case for Johnson but nevertheless the identification of Jesus with personified Wisdom does a number of things. It illustrates the importance of everyday living in the unfolding of the kingdom, and it offers female metaphors as part of the divine process. It also makes inclusion the central element of salvation, that is, those who are normally excluded are counted as friends, accepted, sorted out and loved, not simply tolerated, or worse still forgiven. Jesus, as the child of Sophia, gives hope for the establishment of right relations across all boundaries.[28]

For Johnson the stories of resurrection illustrate how Sophia rises again and again in unimaginable ways, the gift of life cannot be overcome even by extreme torture and death.[29] The disciples are then commissioned to make the inclusive goodness of Sophia 'experientially available'. It could be argued that Christianity is a resurrection faith only when this occurs. As Johnson points out, asserting that Sophia was in Jesus defuses any sexist claims as well as claims to religious exclusivism. Personified Wisdom is at work all over the world and in many different traditions and so Christianity can no longer claim special revelation. Sophia is also inherent in the world and so demands a far greater ecological awareness and striving for balance and right order in the natural world.

While I am not arguing that the Sophia tradition at all does away with a metaphysical understanding of Christ, it does make it difficult to function in a dualistic way, which is half the battle. Sophia as imaged in the Hebrew Bible was in the marketplace with her sleeves rolled up, involved in the everyday life of the people of Israel, and

---

28 Johnson, 'Redeeming the Name of Christ', p. 122.
29 Johnson, 'Redeeming the Name of Christ', p. 124.

this seems to me to be the best starting point for an incarnational religion. It is here too, perhaps, that we can begin to include all stories with no concern about what may over step the mark. Sophia, rather than the Christ of metaphysical absolutes, enables us to read through bodies in order to understand the glorious fullness of divine incarnation. In herself she is not that answer – indeed she points to that lying within us – but she is another way to view the tradition we have inherited and continue to struggle to find a place within. I continue to believe in the embodied importance of christological questioning because once we give ground to metaphysics we are propelled once more into the world of male creation, a place in which women will never find legitimation and self-worth. We need to keep insisting on the bodies of women as a starting point for christological reflection and this raises many interesting questions in relation to sex, sexuality and gender within the wider feminist theology project as we saw in Chapter 1. Feminist theology remains cutting edge and not afraid to face its own internal dilemmas by placing them in the public arena as matters of ongoing debate.

In addition to the question of the place of metaphysics in Christology for the future, feminist theologians still have a number of pressing highly political issues to address and unravel. One question that desperately needs addressing is that of Christian anti-Semitism, which is always a real danger when dealing with Christology. It is a danger because Christianity has had to say something unique about Jesus and this has often involved undervaluing or mis-representing Judaism as a result. Despite our best efforts we, like others before us, have been involved in 'false reading', some of which has had devastating effects. Jewish feminists have for some time been unhappy with the way in which some Christian feminists have uncritically continued to present Jesus as the saviour of women in first-century Palestine. The so-called 'teaching of contempt'[30] has

---

30 Katharina Von Kellenbach, 'Overcoming the Teaching of Contempt', in *A Feminist Companion to Reading the Bible: Approaches, Methods and Strategies*, Athalya Brenner and Carole Fontaine (eds), Sheffield: Sheffield Academic Press, 1997, pp. 41–53.

its roots in the Christian distortion of Judaism, a distortion which portrays Jewish ideals as antithetical to Christian ideals. This has led to a scapegoating of Jews, which in its secular form led to most probably the worst abuses of the twentieth-century: the Holocaust. Feminist theologians have not always learnt from the mistakes of the past and have added another reason for seeing Judaism as inferior: it killed the Goddess and invented patriarchy!

It does appear to be the case that some feminist theologians are suggesting, perhaps unwittingly, that Judaism gave birth to patriarchy and alone killed the goddess. However, more nuanced writers are quite clear that this is not the case. Ruether explains how the male myth took the driving seat over Goddess myths in many near-eastern cultures, not just the Israelite culture; while authors such as Asphodel Long show how the Goddess was never fully eradicated from Judaism, as she was from other near-eastern cultures. Of course, the mistake that we have all I am sure made, is to imply that Judaism is in some way a prologue for Christianity and therefore ceases to be truly valid in the present day. Worse still, that as Christian feminists we can somehow take the bits from the Hebrew scriptures that suit our arguments and interpret them completely in our own context, not paying attention to their historic and cultural roots. Appropriation works towards the elimination of difference and so is essentially a non-feminist activity, but it is something that feminists do.

Christian feminist theology needs to help forge respect for Jews and Judaism and this is done best by giving up ideas of superiority and notions of 'correct readings' when it comes to shared texts like the Hebrew scriptures. This does not mean that any critical engagement has to be shelved in favour of political correctness, but it does mean that Christian feminists need to be sure that this is scholarly and not a mere reinvention of centuries of anti-Semitism. Where does this leave us with Christology, a branch of theology that by its very nature appears to have to give unique status to Jesus? Do we have to imply that Jesus overcame all the shortcomings of Judaism if we are to continue any christological discourse at all? Of course we do if we are going to continue to assert some metaphysical truths about the man. However, if we assume that Christ is an ethical construct, we do move a little further away from condemnation – though are not entirely clear of it. After all, we could still declare that Jesus was ethically superior to anything known by Judaism (this of course is not the case since he owed his ethical and messianic understandings to his own Jewish background). In dispensing with the metaphysical nature of Christ we are also able to ground Jesus more fully in his heritage by doing away with the kind of superman notions that he could miraculously become a man beyond his time. He was a man from his tradition. This, of course, means that we should become well-acquainted with that tradition if we are to base our own understandings of the divine upon it. Rather than distance ourselves from it as some kind of outdated antiquity it should be alive to us as we try to understand the immensity of incarnation, which sprang from the tradition. If we keep insisting on imposing Greek metaphysics on a tradition which was far earthier we will continue to have conflict.

Another blow to the stronghold of Greek metaphysics comes from what Kwok Pui-lan calls 'Jesus the native'.[31] As the colonial Christ fades into the sunset many new faces emerge and they come with an entirely different set of cultural assumptions once they free themselves from western, imperialistic thought. This brings many exciting challenges for Christology because it is exposed to other ways of thinking. What will happen to it in a world where dualistic opposition is simply not accepted and the whole notion of many natures has no place to thrive? How is Christ the Lord to appear to cultures that are not organized along such hierarchical lines? There is an interesting clash of culture when we consider the Aboriginal understanding of land and belonging which presents us with a stark contrast to a timeless and placeless Christ who hovers over all eternity. For Aboriginal people eternity is in the Dreaming, which is

31 See Kwok Pui-lan, 'Jesus the Native', in Fernando F. Segovia and Mary Ann Tolbert (eds), *Teaching the Bible: The Discourse and Politics of Biblical Pedagogy*, Maryknoll: Orbis Books, 1998, pp. 69–85.

both in the past and in the present. It lays down the way that life is and determines patterns of behaviour. The Dreaming also grounds that which is divine in the here and now, not in some transcendent realm. The divine is immanent in the land and in the Dreaming. What does all this say to Christology? Certainly there is no concept of incarnation that can be tied into Aboriginal culture and so Jesus becomes a dreaming hero, one who demands that people be rooted in their land. A figure found in the past and grounding people in the present with little regard for the future, except in as far as it is the time of 'nows'. If Christ is transformed under such a worldview what happens to the eschatological promises?

Kwok Pui-Lan alerts us to the way the Bible is read and thus the Christ who emerges from it – she claims it is still a European activity and so the Christ who emerges still has a very European feel to him. She is not at all surprised by this since she understands the quest for the historical Jesus as setting the scene for control of knowledge. She claims that just as westerners of the day went in search of the authentic 'native' so they went in search of the authentic Jesus, in order to own and control both.[32] Kwok does not consider it to be an accident that in the United States there was renewal of the search for the historical Jesus during the Reagan–Bush era, a time of political conservatism. While the first quest grew during a time of colonial expansion the second, she argues, grew when questions of immigration and national identity were hot political questions. Once again white would-be rulers used the christological discourse to assert their own uniqueness and dominance. Jesus the native presents feminist theology with yet another challenge, which is how to move beyond Eurocentric methods without patronizing any particular group. The answer does not entirely lie in beginning from experience, because once experience is theorized the methods are once again western. Indeed, the constructs themselves are western, such as time and dualism.

We are at a very exciting time in the christological story since we

---

32 Kwok Pui-lan, 'Jesus the Native', p. 77.

are able to view the discipline through so many lenses. Indeed, the acceptance of process thought and parts of postmodernism have enabled us to begin to question the meaning and use of metaphysics within the christological debate. Through the opening of theology to experience once more – and we should not forget that theology was at the beginning a reflection on experience of the divine – we have made it possible to not only question the meaning of such notions as the Suffering Servant but also to question the foundation stones of Christology itself. The introduction of diverse cultures on their own terms into this arena will, I have no doubt, provide a richer and deeper understanding of the nature of incarnation.

Possibly the greatest contribution that feminist theology has made in this area is to insist that Christology remains ethical, that is it has to be judged by outcomes and not simply by internal logic. As an undergraduate all those years ago, Christology was an exercise in understanding the disclosure of the nature and significance of Jesus through the ages, this significance rarely had anything to do with politics of the radical and inclusive kind. We have come a long way and as a pilgrim people we have further to go.

5

Life After Death

Feminist theologies have often been accused of ignoring parts of the Christian tradition that could, conceivably, cause them problems. With its materialist leanings and its suspicion of anything dualistic and even for some metaphysical (see Chapter 4), it is clear why matters such as the afterlife would have very little appeal on the agenda of theologians engaged in a radical critique of patriarchal theorizing. However it remains the case that for many who work in feminist theology the matter is far from simple, and so the controversies rumble on over whether we live after death and, if so, how? As feminist and body theologians the question is an interesting one because is it really possible to say that the body carries so much theological significance and then simply ceases to be? One day it is here at the heart of theological revolution and the next it is in a grave and of no further significance at all. Of course this is not what all feminist theologians are saying, even those who do not argue for a life after death. The way in which feminist theology approaches this is more subtle than its detractors would give it credit for. What appears to have become destabilized is the rhetoric that places heaven as a stick with which to beat the wayward and a place for the continuation of the ego for those whose sense of self is so contained within the edges of their own skin. In this way the critique of the afterlife by feminist theologians is a welcome move in these days of crushing capitalism and the conforming characters it depends so completely upon. Of course there are those who argue that in this world, where exploitation and premature death remains a reality for the majority, the promise of heaven must be a good thing since it gives some kind of meaning to what would otherwise appear entirely unjust and meaningless. But there again, lack of such a promise may place the weight of changing unjust systems squarely on the shoulders of those who create or tolerate them, leading to a utopian vision being worked for not simply believed in. As previously stated this is a complex issue and one that Christian feminist theologies can tackle from within a rich biblical tradition.

Belief in life after death was widespread in the ancient world and the Hebrew scriptures provide us with a variety of responses to the problem. The Semitic worldview was rather different from our own seeing the cosmos as divided into three layers: earth, heaven and the netherworld. This enabled a belief that those in either the higher (gods) or lower (the dead) regions could intervene in human affairs. To die simply meant to change one's place in the cosmic structure, so that while there was physical decay something of the person remained – personality traits and memory for example (1 Samuel 28.10–14). The quality of life that one had after death depended on the life led on earth and the vigilance of one's children in carrying out rituals. The dead either resided in the lighter, upper parts of Sheol or the lower more squalid parts (Isaiah 14.4–21). Those who resided in the upper parts were given the title 'gods' (1 Samuel 28.13; Psalm 16.3) as they could intervene in people's lives in startling ways. Private rituals were carried out to keep the dead happy and to ensure they remained in the upper regions of Sheol where they could be most effective for the living.

The later biblical writers condemned ancestor worship and speaking to the dead at the same time as advocating the worship of the one true God. This was possibly as much to do with attempting to create a national identity under pressure from outside forces as it was to do with theological insight. The outcome of these condemnations was that the living and the dead became totally separated and the bodies of the dead were viewed as unclean. The dead were seen as existing in a dark and gloomy place but at least they were free from the trials of the earth (Job 3.17–19). However, there is also the notion that once removed from life people were also removed from the worship of Yahweh (Sirach 17.22f), they were godless and alone. In fact as the religion of Yahweh developed death came to be seen as the end of being. However, this belief saw a turn-around and once again political expectation and theology interacted to produce a belief in the resurrection of the body. While the nation itself was gradually being wiped off the map the people nevertheless clung to the promises of God that they would be a great nation. Their hope for liberation coupled with their encounter with Zoroastrian religion led to a new hope. Between 585 and 568 BCE Ezekiel delivered a series of hope-filled visions in which he saw a New Jerusalem and the dry bones of the dead raised to life. Some scholars have argued that the Zoroastrian influence on this vision was more direct than may have been imagined over the years. The plain of dry bones that Ezekiel claims to have seen may actually have been a Zoroastrian burial ground since it was the practice of Zoroastrians to leave bodies to be devoured by birds and the bones to be bleached by the sun. They believed that the creator would reassemble the bones at the final resurrection. Ezekiel no doubt knew of this belief but nevertheless he used it for his own purposes. Whereas Zoroastrians expected a renewed universe Ezekiel looked for a New Jerusalem with the people free from foreign oppression.[1] So while taking over the belief he also made it more parochial in nature by seeing it only in terms of the New Jerusalem – a backward step, perhaps, in terms of political ideology. It is not entirely clear whether Ezekiel thought this resurrection would last for ever but others who came later believed that it had a limited time span; for example, Enoch thought it lasted 500 years and then people died again (1 Enoch 10.10). Despite its non-eternal quality this kind of resurrection still helped people make sense of their present suffering and their apparently unconcerned God. So even in the very early days there is a move heavenward in order to convince people of a caring God who will intervene even after death in order to bring some equity to an otherwise hard to

---

1 C. McDannell and B. Lang, *Heaven: A History*, London: Yale University Press, 1988, pp. 12–13.

fathom world. It is interesting that even a 500-year extension period of life in another realm seems to satisfy this sense of justice-making.

There were those in the Hebrew Bible who appeared to deny death altogether such as Elijah and Enoch who were assumed bodily into heaven. It was their example that is taken up in Psalm 73 with the author musing that what is possible for those holy men is possible for all. Thus residing with God in heaven rather than languishing in Sheol became a real hope for all. The idea had entered the religious arena that ones relationship with God, if it were strong enough, could not be broken by death. This highlights the importance of the individual in the development of Jewish thought, marking a move from corporate identity and development of the notion of individual punishment or reward. While Jewish thought emphasized the relationship between God and the people as a whole there was no need for the idea of life after death with reward or punishment for the individual, but once the relationship became more personal, because justice was not seen to be done to the deserving race, what happened to the individual after death became a more pressing matter. We notice in these days the emphasis placed on life after death appears to be more extreme with the more right-wing Protestant groups. Indeed, many of these groups declare that Christianity is only of any consequence if Jesus himself rose from the dead and thereby promises life everlasting to those who follow him. Given that the message of his ministry seemed to be about justice it is odd to muse why this should be seen as THE important point of a life such as his. There again, perhaps we are seeing the idea of justice writ large in terms of those who believe they are good wanting to have some reward for it beyond the run of the mill. What we are witnessing is a religion with a strong sense of individualism emphasizing individual life after death – not a new phenomenon.

Jewish thought was not immune to Greek influence and we witness an increasing concern with the nature of the soul. The book of Wisdom took it for granted that the soul exists and is strong in determining who we actually are, while Philo of Alexandria developed his thinking to the point of understanding this life as just a brief and unfortunate interlude that interrupts the true higher existence of the soul. Many souls lose their way in the material world but the true ones reach a higher immortal state.[2] The unfortunate consequence of this was that there was no interest any longer in nationalism and the resurrection of the state but rather personal 'soul preparation' took the place of political action. By the time Christianity emerged there was a rich variety of thought available on the subject of the afterlife, and it is as well to remember that the understanding of the early Jesus movement would have been formed in this world with its conflicting ideas and aims.

It is therefore not extraordinary that early Christianity would have views on this matter and that they may even appear to differ with author and region. We are immediately faced with a stark and challenging statement in Romans 1.3-4 where we are told that it was the resurrection that turned Jesus of Nazareth into the Christ. It is this statement that influences those Christians who claim that without the resurrection there can be no Christianity. As the same Christians also cling to the Virgin Birth as a sign of the divine nature of the man Jesus we can see just how important the resurrection and its promise of eternal life is felt to be – it is the validating point of an otherwise unremarkable event: the virgin birth and life of Jesus! Surprising then that the Gospels do not pay more attention to the matter of life after death, especially as it was such a hot topic in the world in which they took form.

Jesus is also reported as having no interest in what happens to dead bodies which suggests that the body was not essential for eternal life. However, we are also faced with the resurrection stories which are at pains to point out that Jesus has risen from the dead and is still in his body. Although he is reported to have the ability to appear through walls and doors (John 20.26), and is often not instantly recognizable (John 21.1-14), he can be touched and does still bear the scars received at death as well as appearing to still have a healthy appetite. Of course after his appearances Jesus ascended

---

2 McDannell and Lang, *Heaven: A History*, p. 17.

into heaven and it is unclear whether he kept his body despite having ascended with it. So there is much here to feed the theological imagination.

A significant contribution was made to the debate by Paul who as a Pharisee had certain ideas already. He put forward the concept that at death the person sleeps and at a later time would be reunited with God. The dead would be bodily resurrected and enjoy life in a kingdom where God rules eternally. The resurrected bodies are, however, spiritual. Those who are alive at the time of the final judgement will be transformed into spiritual beings in the twinkling of an eye. Paul is unclear as to how these bodies would look, but he is very clear that heaven involves dwelling in the presence of God for ever. Paul has, of course, a very interesting theology of the cross, which is in fact linked with the theology of resurrection. For him the cross is a sign of the process of transformation and redemption, a process that all have to enter into if they are also to enter the resurrection with Christ. In a real sense for Paul it is the resurrection of the body that is its final goal, that is to say, its innate destiny (1 Cor. 15.35–55). It is the logical and necessary continued process of change that gives the body its true meaning and in a sense gives the true meaning to the life of Christ. Why else would the divine take flesh other than to open up for all what is truly their divine destiny by leading the way in the fulfilling process of the human body we, and the divine, inhabit? Life after death, in whatever form it may take, is the destiny of the human body redeemed and set free from the slavery of living a deceived life. It is the fullness of human existence. Indeed we can see why such a way of thinking is appealing; there is logic here as well as a sense of meaning, although justice is less obvious as it could be argued that all are included in this extended life.

When we move forward to the Fathers we see an emerging picture in relation to bodily resurrection which they saw as necessary for a number of reasons. Aquinas argued that we are not really people if we do not have bodies, which is a very interesting line of argument to follow and is indeed one that is current today among those who advocate life after death and the resurrection of the body. Tertullian, on the other hand, maintained that justice demands that we are judged as a whole with the implication being that reward or punishment needed a body in which to enact itself. His extended thinking on this matter was based in an interesting view of nature – he claimed that nature, in fact, demands resurrection since it is made for humans and is continually renewed. Therefore it would be nonsense to suggest that humans could perish as nature keeps blooming for us.[3] This line of argument would be highly contested today by feminist theologians and others as a rather self-centred and inaccurate way of viewing the purpose of nature. While we may wish to applaud his attempts at understanding the continuation of human life in relation to nature, his way of doing it is as androcentric as most patristic theology and flawed as a result. If we are to understand ourselves and nature side by side then it has to be in terms of our own innate place and not viewing nature as here to serve us. This gift of ecofeminist thinking allows us to think differently not only about our place while alive but also our place after death as we shall see.

The Fathers presumed that the resurrection of the flesh was taught throughout the Bible and as we have seen this is not wholly correct. Therefore we have to question this part of our Christian heritage, or at least see it in a new light. Of course, as with all traditions, what we inherit is not uniform or monotraditional for example, despite their insistence on the resurrection of the body, the Fathers also agreed that this was nothing compared to the bliss that believers would eventually have in heaven. So we could say that resurrection of the body was to be here on earth and a further resurrection perhaps beyond the body in heaven was to occur. There is ambiguity as we saw in the biblical accounts of what was believed to happen to Jesus body after the transfiguration. For some such as Augustine in the *City of God*, resurrection is understood as restoration of bodily wholeness with the added bonus of incorruptibility.

---

3 Paul Badham, *Christian Beliefs About Life After Death*, London: MacMillan, 1976, pp. 53–4.

For him the thirteenth-century introduction of the practice of dissecting saints and burying their parts in different places would have caused a theological problem perhaps. At the same time as this introduction two councils, the fourth Lateran and Lyon, were affirming that all rise with the bodies that they now wear! This would leave God with a huge reassembling task and logic would dictate that keeping body parts together was the best solution.

However, Augustine thought that we did rise as a whole and had an idea of how that would be. He declared that we would rise aged 30, gendered and whole with an added possibility that the most virtuous would be transparent to show off their harmoniously arranged livers and intestines.[4] In a sense the extended period of life ushers in the complete harmony that Christianity was thought to encompass. I am always tempted to see this move as a note of realism or perhaps lack of faith, on behalf of theologians who on the one hand declare Christianity to be a world-transforming way of life and on the other declare that it is all made complete after death and in another realm. Albeit for some that realm is a transformed and almost unrecognizable earth. There seems something incongruous about an incarnational religion advocating a realm that is removed that somehow puts everything right. This appears to be rather a different argument from that of the desire for justice which was considered earlier, it is rather an extension period in which all the failings of the flesh can be eradicated and the body will shine in glory. There really does not seem too much justification for such an argument in incarnational theology which declares the human–divine existence to be inseparable. Flesh in and of itself seems to be a generous enough host for the divine and here seems to be where that process of wholeness and completion is signalled as taking place.

A fair amount of the Christian heritage shows a fear of people being swallowed by the natural processes of decay. Death, in much

---

4 Caroline Walker Bynum, *The Resurrection of the Body in Western Christianity, 200–1336*, New York: Columbia University Press, 1995, p. 100.

of the Christian tradition, was seen as disgusting as it meant that people had surrendered uncontrollably to the functions of the body. A body that was often viewed with suspicion anyway by certain elements of the tradition. Further, there was a fear that people could not keep their personality if there was not a body to attach it to. Hildegard, however, conveys the idea that there can be organic change without threat to the self.[5] Do we see the beginning of a feminist critique of patriarchal theology with her views on the matter of life after death? This twelfth-century polymath places before us an organic image of the human person that is not at all threatened by the notion of change and decay. As a medical practitioner she easily accepted the idea that something organic can change and still remain itself, even that alien substances can be incorporated into the organic make-up with no threat to who we are. She goes further, insisting that human kind is not true to itself when it does not in fact change through the giving forth and the taking in of all that is within the world. She does speak about the soul as the enlivener of the body, but even the body itself is understood as essentially human and of value in its composition of earth, mud and ashes. Combined with the fact that she rarely speaks of the end things one may be encouraged to believe that she was indeed a proto-feminist challenging the dualistic division of heaven and earth. However, as ever when looking back to our foresisters we need to proceed with caution. Hildegard does mention the problems that may be encountered if God is considering reassembling scattered bodies and one wonders if there is a hint of sarcasm here. However, she goes on to assert that people are raised in two sexes without former deformities and she speaks of glorified bodies as 'light' and worthy vehicles of fiery souls. It remains true that she says very little at all about heaven as though her theology of process and fertility has no place for such an endpoint which may appear rather static by comparison. Given her developed notion of the person as a psychosomatic unity she is faced with a difficulty in relation to her theology of growth – the body decays and

---

5 Walker Bynum, *The Resurrection of the Body*, p. 159.

so what of growth? For her a resurrected body has to be able to carry the thrust of change and process that she understands as so central to the nature of humankind – so she speaks of such bodies but, as already said, there is no talk of heaven. So maybe not a modern feminist! But what are we to make of her ideas of growth and organic wholeness? Can they be seen at least in a trajectory with some modern feminist thinking – were the problems there for her and the options narrower?

Whatever our conclusion regarding Hildegard's position we see that Christian feminist liberation theologians have a varied and rich tradition to consider. Despite this not a great deal has been written about life after death possibly because the problems of this world have seemed paramount. Indeed, as already mentioned, some feel that the problems of this world are not helped, indeed may be formed, by a western notion that things do not have to work out here since there is a beyond in which justice prevails. There could be some avoidance of this topic in the hope that by moving to the solutions, regarding the big problems, the theology will follow, in this case a rethink over the issue of life after death. It is true to say that when the topic of life after death has been approached it has been with extreme caution due to the implicit dualistic logic that underpins such theology.

Heyward is a feminist theologian who has been very careful to avoid dualistic thinking when dealing with resurrection and life after death. Indeed, in her whole christological project, she situates Jesus within the material world more than the spiritual. Her reimaging allows us to see that it is the human Jesus who is our greatest advocate since it then becomes through human capacity that God may be incarnate in the world. Heyward makes much of the sense of growth into divinity hinted at in Luke and she sees this as the way in which we are all invited into transforming relationship with God. She argues that once we value the humanity of Jesus, we breach the dualistic gulf between God and humanity. And, of course, create large problems in relation to traditional views of resurrection and life after death! If humans do not, in the natural course of things, resurrect or are seen to have life after death, how can this human son of God change that pattern without some very extra-human activity? On the other hand, if this is a man who is growing into his divine nature and succeeds beyond any other to date, then why should he not in fact resurrect and have life after death – why should this not be the way we can all go if we too live our divine natures to the same depth?

In some ways we may see an outworking here of Hildegard's organic theology, it may be said that the natural end of the fully alive human, who is infused with the love of God, is eternal life. However, before the evangelicals get too excited there seems to be an implication in Heyward that this is not a given but rather something we have to work out in the real material substance of our own lives in the here and now – so not for everyone then. Although Heyward does not say much about resurrection she is adamant that whatever it is and however we perceive it we should not develop a way of thinking that allows us to lessen the impact of the terrible torture and death through the 'glory of the resurrection'. This she sees as being a deeply troubling mistake in some Christian theology. For Heyward the resurrection is what happens to those who align themselves with the praxis of Jesus and stubbornly refuse to give up intimacy and immediacy with God.[6] It is something that happens in this life and she is really unclear about whether it continues in some form after death. The uniqueness of Christians calling themselves a resurrection people lies for her in their assertion that they hold fast to intimacy with God and make it again and again in the face of destruction and despair. It is this movement that she believes we see with the early followers who, despite their devastation at the manner and death of Jesus, felt his presence and carried on the life they had dedicated themselves to – no guarantee here of a reward in heaven for Heyward.

While we have to admit that Heyward herself is open on this

---

6 See Lisa Isherwood, *Liberating Christ*, Cleveland, OH: Pilgrim Press, 1999, p. 100.

question, we can see through the way that she develops her Christology that a God who rescues Jesus and the holy to heaven and to life ever after is rather cruel: he watches suffering and does nothing, only taking some at the end to a better realm. Why not act sooner and stop the suffering, one feels compelled to ask. In addition, the Christology Heyward places before us does not make us feel that resurrection needs to be the final trick in order to validate the life of Jesus. This stands as it is as a glorious invitation to divine life without the need of conjuring tricks and worlds apart.

Rosemary Radford Ruether is among those who believe it to be of fundamental importance that we give up notions of eternal survival,[7] since this androcentric obsession has almost caused the destruction of the world. Many Christian feminists are highly suspicious of eschatology, arguing that in its most individualistic form it reflects a particularly male concern with the independent, isolated self and has contributed towards the ecological crisis. This is a theme that has been taken up by Catherine Keller when she argues that this end-time thinking places us in the predicament that we wish to escape by a living out of all we really wish to avoid, there is an unending cycle that needs to be broken by thinking otherwise.[8] She would in part agree with Ruether who says,

by pretending that we can immortalize ourselves, our souls, and perhaps even our bodies for some future resurrection, we are immortalizing our garbage and polluting the earth. If we are really to learn to recycle our garbage as fertiliser for new growth, our waste as matter for new artefacts, we need a spirituality of recycling that accepts ourselves as part of that process of growth, decay, reintegration into the earth and new growth.[9]

---

7 Rosemary Radford Ruether 'Ecofeminism and Healing Ourselves, Healing the Earth', *Feminist Theology* Vol. 9, Sheffield: Sheffield Academic Press, 1995, pp. 51–62.

8 Catherine Keller, *Apocalypse Now and Then*, Boston: Beacon Press, 1996.

9 Ruether, 'Ecofeminism and Healing Ourselves', p. 61.

Where she may part company with Ruether is that she believes that even the anti-end-time thinking holds within it something of the end-time thinking which is so destructive. We need to be far more creative than we have to date managed to be when we think of what happens next to the good and the not so good.

For Ruether the answer lies in seeing human consciousness as part of this process of disintegration, returning to 'a great consciousness underlying the whole of the life process that carries and expands with the remembering of each of our small selves, while letting go of the illusion of immortal self within each of our many moral embodiments'.[10] There is no sense here of human beings falling into nothingness. Rather human beings move from one form of existence into another, one form of embodiment to another, in the body of God. Salvation ceases to be a matter for the next world and becomes instead a matter of flourishing in this world.[11] There are hints of Hildegard here with the notion of flourishing and organic growth that seems to underpin what Ruether is suggesting. Like Hildegard, Ruether is looking for an ecologically sound and coherent way of understanding the place of the human within the cosmos and she does not find it helpful, or indeed convincing, to see our fulfilment lying in a removal from the ground that formed us and the stuff from which we are made. There is a profound understanding of incarnation at play here which will not let go when faced with what seems an unanswerable question of what happens when we die. Ruether wants us to face our fears and our desires for immortality and to see them for what they are – vain glory, but much worse than that, ideas that make us vulnerable to ideologies that ruin the earth, seeing it and us as a renewable divine resource.

There are great dangers in simply accepting a view of life after death that also includes a renewed planet on which to dwell as can be seen by those politicians and business men who advocate using all

---

10 Ruether 'Ecofeminism and Healing Ourselves', p. 61.

11 See Grace Jantzen, *Power, Gender and Christian Mysticism*, Cambridge: Cambridge University Press, 1995.

the resources of the planet in order that Christ will return all the quicker and we will dwell with God all the sooner. However, as dangerous as this is, we still have to ask whether Ruether's approach adequately accounts for an embodied longing for immortality in God. When asked, the average person in the street is most likely to say that they believe in life after death even when they do not believe in other aspects of religion. As Elizabeth Stuart points out,[12] if we claim that feminist theology takes account of people's experience, then we have to take notice of such surveys especially if the respondents offer some experience of those who have died. Of course it does not mean that we have to conclude there is life after death, but rather that the human personality is so estranged from its true core that it feels fear and the desire for some reassurance, or indeed that we cannot cope with the loss of a loved one and so carry on the hope of meeting despite all the evidence to the contrary. In short, such surveys may simply provide us with excellent questions for research into the psychological nature of humans and tell us very little about spiritual realms beyond what we see. Nevertheless we do well to heed Stuart's question. Ruether is representative of the views of many feminist theologians but we still have to ask whether these views are an adequate reinterpretation of the tradition's emphasis on the continuity and discontinuity for the resurrected body, whether they offer a sufficiently embodied account of life after death, and whether they fail to take account of the life-experience of those who, because of social, economic and ecological situations, die young and have no chance to flourish, unlike most western middle-class people. In other words, does this only work for those who can expect to live long and relatively trouble-free lives – is it just another western construct?

Elizabeth Stuart is concerned that feminist theologians who place so much store on the body and relationality simply see the body

---

12 Elizabeth Stuart, 'Elizabeth Stuart Phelps: A Good Woman Doing Bad Theology', *Feminist Theology*, 26, Sheffield: Sheffield Academic Press, 2001, pp. 70–82.

ultimately as wastage, to be recycled, but not into anything that is recognizable.[13] This she sees as declaring, despite much rhetoric to the contrary, that embodiment and relationality have no real value and that we accept a certain fatalism and an implicit notion of natural wastage. Stuart says, 'to buy into a theo-ecological model of redemption is actually to be prepared to suffer (albeit with pain and regret) such waste; it is to say that ultimately individual lives have no value to the divine except as some kind of recycled food'.[14] She asks if those who create the most garbage actually feel their guilt relieved by seeing themselves as waste to be recycled as well. Of course there is a world of difference between waste and recycling and Ruether, and perhaps Hildegard before her, does not see the recycling model as one of natural wastage at all. It can be argued that in the 'divine compost' approach we continue to be co-creators with the divine through the reintegration of our bodies into the earth, through the continued relationality of those decaying bodies with the earth around them and the absorption of the atoms that formed us into the ether and beyond into new forms and continued life. What this approach does is guard against a precious individualism that can be easily translated into life-denying and ego-serving theology before death. I think it is, in fact, taking bodies and relationality extremely seriously and asking the question about consciousness and relationality that we are only on the edge of being able to answer through the everyday unfolding of the mysteries of quantum physics. The Jesus of the tradition is shown to us as undergoing many transformations, why should we not see our own inevitable rearrangement through decay of this flesh as a continued journey that does not require the 'I' that I know but rather a continued relationality that changes with the shift in composition?

Stuart is not content to challenge the nuts and bolts of feminist positions on life after death, she also challenges what she sees as a political giving of ground. In depriving itself of heaven she believes

---

13 Stuart, 'Elizabeth Stuart Phelps', p. 79.
14 Stuart, 'Elizabeth Stuart Phelps', p. 80.

feminist theology has damned itself 'to the unforgiving and suffocating present'.[15] It has done away with a useful space in which to play and to gain a different perspective on the past and the present, in this way to create a new future. By conceding the otherworld to patriarchy Stuart claims that feminist theologians have thickened the material order 'so that no other reality can survive within it'.[16] For Stuart this has liturgical implications also seeing as she does the Eucharist in particular, quoting Ratzinger, as

> a rehearsal of the life to come, a form of play in which we learn about and prepare for a life which St Augustine describes, by contrast with life in this world, as a fabric woven, no longer of exigency and need, but of the freedom of generosity and gift.[17]

In the Eucharist we step into the space between heaven and earth, a space that Stuart claims has to be there in any form of process theology, which is why she criticizes feminist theologians for giving it up. If the world is in the process of becoming, she claims, then it has to be acknowledged that it is not there yet and so needs the idea of an end and a liturgical life to remind us what we are striving for. In addition the sense of mystery that is involved in liturgy is abandoned by those who would see a more organic end to humankind.

For Stuart the whole sense of mystery involved with sacramental life and the whole liturgical order itself in some way requires the idea of the afterlife and in return it offers a way of thinking beyond patriarchy. For her, what she views as a liberal Protestant approach, to life after death has conceded too much of the Christian life to patriarchy. Stuart argues that the life after death that the Eucharist rehearses is a very queer one indeed and so she is challenging feminist theology through an engagement with queer theology. Her claim is that through the Eucharist all things are transformed and the

---

15 Stuart, 'Elizabeth Stuart Phelps', p. 80.

16 Elizabeth Stuart, 'Exploding Mystery: Feminist Theology and the Sacramental', *Feminist Theology*, Vol. 12.2, London: Continuum, 2004, pp. 228–36.

17 Stuart, 'Exploding Mystery', p. 234.

dead are keeping company with the living, even the edges of existence are changed. Further, there is real political might in this
arrangement of the cosmos since our fights for justice can be fuelled
by the knowledge that 'angels and archangels and the whole company of heaven' are with us,[18] and so we cannot despair and we
cannot ultimately lose. Stuart is keen to make it known that we are
expected to struggle for justice here and not take satisfaction in the
reality of heaven.

When we consider Stuart's thought we realize that in challenging
and reshaping the notion of life after death feminist theologians have
challenged so much more besides. It has to be said that some of
those who reject the traditional notions of life after death still find
much meaning in liturgy and even the Eucharist understanding it as
a communal, relational statement of intent more than one of rehears-
ing existing heavens. Stuart may be right that liturgy is important as
it introduces us to mystery but those who reject life after death do
not necessarily see the mystery of the world at once collapsed.
Indeed it may be argued that the mystery of the here and now and the
fragility of life which adds to that depth of awe and wonder are
increased by the nowness of the relational experience. Dualistic
metaphysics have not served women or the planet well and it can of
course be argued that this is simply because they have been misused
in the hands of patriarchy. This may be true, it is almost impossible
to say, but what we can say is that the distance and hierarchy they
have created have played a large part in the exploitative nature of the
western world. If by challenging these efficient bedfellows, we are
also thrown into questioning the other world they create and the
promises of extended self-interest beyond, then this is a good thing.
After all we can do no more than question and suggest outcomes that
may spring from a new way of thinking – can we know anything in
this matter? Of course not, we simply have to spend time observing
behaviours and outcomes, this takes generations and so each theological act is then an act of faith.

---

18 Stuart, 'Exploding Mystery', p. 236.

It does, however, seem that once we abandon the illusions of dualism and unchanging absolutes we are in a healthier position. That is, we no longer have to fear change as being outside the realm of the divine, in fact it is the nature of the divine. Change is holy and we should embrace it rather than trying to halt what is natural by appealing to intellectual tricks. This has quite significant outcomes in the here and now for women and indeed for all those whose bodies are subject to change and decay. Certainly this is a human condition but we have in hiding from our own change, and decay has been harsh on those whose bodies are seen to be different through illness and disease. Embracing change as a part of an organic notion of death will have a positive influence on other aspects of theologies of the body also. If we move to seeing death as merely reintegration of our body into the earth, a very physical merging with the energy that we have called divine, but without any sense of personal identity or 'me-ness' continuing, we also find ourselves raising questions about the way in which people are seen to have worth and identity in the here and now. There is no doubt that our western cultures have developed a very overactive sense of the individual self and the whole economic and social order reflects that with devastating consequences in the lives of people. Once we begin to break down the belief that this individualism carries on after death, then we have a chance of changing the way the West organizes itself.

Even those feminist theologians who would challenge life after death very strongly for political as well as theological reasons may not all wish to give up the powerful symbol of resurrection which has spoken to us in various guises down the ages. Many would prefer to see it as an urgent and embodied requirement in the here and now to see it as a symbol for the transformation of the cosmos and the ruptured experiences of people that we as Christians are called to work for. It stands for the business of creating a new heaven and earth in the now, as an unwillingness to give up on divine intimacy in the face of the many crucifixions we see around us daily. There is a definite priority given to a more communal notion of resurrection than individual salvation in most feminist theologies. This as we have seen is not completely out of line with our biblical heritage but does challenge those ideas formed under the weight of Greek dualistic thinking. Perhaps part of the biblical heritage that we can claim when offering a community view of resurrection is that of the women at the cross who remained vigilant throughout the pain and the hopelessness. They wept, mourned, grieved and hurt and in so doing they ushered in a new dawn, a new hope and a new way to imagine the world and to live. This may be the meaning of resurrection in feminist theology. Perhaps feminist theology is going back to ancient biblical concepts or just reading the signs of the times, but personal salvation is not of the utmost importance in the world as we see it today, cosmic resurrection is, and it is a task we all have to undertake as co-redeemers of creation. Our 'reward' in this – is it life after death and a place in heaven? Well, in a way it is life after death, after ours that is, because the greatest reward in a relational, co-creational, co-redemptive theology has to be to have lived in such a way that 'the children's teeth are not set on edge'.

6

Controversies on the Future of Feminist Theologies

In the past ten years conferences and articles about the future of feminist theologies have been abundant and the arguments presented for and against its continuation have varied greatly. Some have had more force than others: some have considered that feminism has not declined but has come to occupy a different position. The so-called 'new wave' of feminism deals with difference, for instance, instead of equality. Interestingly enough feminist theologians, by working on principles of gender justice based on diversity and inclusivity have continuously worked hard at a praxis which goes from dealing with domestic violence to issues of women's ordination. The early accusations of theologians of the developing world concerning the 'whiteness'[1] of feminist theology have been overcome long ago by a postcolonial analysis which shows how the South can also misconstruct the North at times. Stereotypes are not a privilege of the North Atlantic circles of theology. Postcolonial analysis emphasizes the internalization of oppression but also the negotiations performed by women to become not just victims, but precisely to subvert the gender structures of their time. In recent decades, when feminist and liberation theologies have been declared moribund, together with socialism and anything else that does not represent the ideals of the

---

1 See Rosemary Radford Ruether's criticism of the concept of 'white-feminists' (as one word) in the 'Panel III: Feminist Theology II', Religion and the Feminist Movement Conference at Harvard Divinity School in November 2002 (http://www.hds.harvard.edu/wsrp/scholarhip/rfmc/rfm_video.html).

global expansion of capitalism and theologies of the market, we have witnessed an eruption of even more radical feminist theologies. These have been theologies not only representing the experiences of women who have been left behind historically by churches and theology, in general, but even more interesting than that, theologies which have brought with them new methodologies and a conceptually alternative framework of analysis.

For some critics if there has been a fault it lies perhaps in their theological creativity: feminist theologies have become too fragmented to be effective. Strategically, homogenization may sometimes work, as when pooling all the strength of communities towards some common project and interest. But for other critics, feminist theologies are not fragmented enough and still need to overcome hegemonic styles of thinking inherited from Christian traditions. This last criticism can be found especially among feminist religious scholars. For instance, Rita Gross has made the criticism that the term 'feminist theology' seems to refer only to Christian theology.[2] That may be true up to a point but developing world and postcolonial theologies especially, not to mention the diverse spectrum of queer theology, not only reflect the perspectives of other religious traditions but have also redefined Christian theology in more ample terms.[3]

---

2 See Gross's article, 'Where Have We Been? Where Do We Need to Go?: Women's Studies and Gender in Religion and Feminist Theology', in Ursula King and Tina Beattie (eds) *Gender, Religion and Diversity: Cross Cultural Perspectives*, London: Continuum, 2004, p. 27. Gross advocates a more religiously diverse focus for feminist theologies in general.

3 See, for instance, the work of Randy Conner on African religion such as Santería and Umbanda which are somehow part of the Christian popular traditions of Latin America in Randy Conner, *Queering Creole Spiritual Traditions*, New York: Harrington Park Press, 2004. The whole thealogy research goes outside the limits of Christianity and the work of postcolonial feminist theologians such as Kwok Pui-Lan and Musa Dube interrogates Christianity in relation to other religions. Also it is important to consider here the work done by The Circle of Concerned African Theologians.

However, if there is a more controversial issue, it is that of the demands of having a very experiential, focused theological reflection (for instance, a Dalit or a Filipina theology[4]) while maintaining a plural framework. That is, there is the challenge of having a class, gender, sexual, political and cultural analysis in each reflection, even if the community is not particularly interested in any of these aspects. In a way it is as if each theological position demands that its own issues should be central also for other reflections. Thus for womanists, race is the central theme, the hermeneutical key which also provides them with their critical analysis; while in Latin America it would be more common to find a class-based analysis. Sexuality, for instance, is normally left to women who are not heterosexuals: as if heterosexuality did not also deserve its own ideological questionings. Why is it necessary to have this integral framework of analysis? Should white women use womanist and Latina's tools, while womanists use also class analysis from their neighbour liberationists in Latin America? Should the pioneer feminist theologians who have contributed so much to feminist hermeneutics, dedicate themselves to reflect on bisexuality or trans-gender theologies? At a superficial level it might be thought that being bisexual, or being black, or from an Asian culture is not where they are coming from: there is an issue of experience to be taken into account. Perhaps if one never lived in a country with a rich multifaith life and a tradition of goddesses, one might claim that this is not the right point of departure for doing feminist theology: it should be from the critical reality of their communities which are involved in struggle. That may be true and perhaps that is the reason why men

---

4 Dalit women theology deals with the particular concerns of the Dalits as a scheduled caste in India. For further references see, for instance, Mary Grey, *The Unheard Scream: The Struggles of Dalit Women in India*, New Dehli: Centre for Dalit/Subaltern Studies, 2004. WomenFilipina theology has specific characteristics of political analysis, militancy for social changes, post-colonial and interfaith reflections. See, for instance, the pioneer work from Sr Mary Jo Mananzan and the reflections of a new generation of Filipina theologians such as Gemma Tulud Cruz.

do not engage in feminist theology (or any gender/sexual based theology, except queer and gay theologians).

However, there are close ideological connections between, for instance, religious colonial identities and gender, sexuality, race and class. Feminist methodological perspectives do not operate in isolation from each other but, on the contrary, tend to illuminate each other. A feminist critical theory requires multiple analyses to understand the crossroads and intersections of power and the structures of oppression. Yet it will be difficult in practice to find a feminist theological work which includes all these dimensions of analysis in the same depth. The controversy arises not only because for some women some issues are more relevant than others, but also because some women are in disagreement with the concerns of other women. They may not approve of bisexuality, for instance, or consider perhaps that race is not a relevant locus for doing theology. In feminist theologies, as in other disciplines, what theologians are silent about may mean indifference – but never neutrality.

To discuss the future or dismissal of feminist theology itself, at a time when many women find it difficult to identify with a label such as 'feminist theologians' is also complex. The 'labelling game' may have changed. Are we still feminist or not? The term 'feminist' in itself has come to mean a multitude of, if not contradictory then different, positions. Many still use the term to refer to the first wave of feminism, which as has been said, emphasized radical equality. That has been replaced by the paradigm of difference. Liberal feminists differ from, say, socialist feminists. Also, feminism has been diversified and enriched by postmodernism and by postcolonialism. We may be even confronting a postfeminist generation of theologians who, although still described under the umbrella of 'feminist theology', have substantial differences in their theoretical approaches, goals and tasks from previous generations. Somehow queer theologians have managed to complicate things even further. It is not just women who are the subject of the discourse but people questioning the imposition of heterosexual ideologies upon theology. Gay and lesbian, transvestite and bisexual, transgender and transsexual theologians are part of the increasingly deeper questioning of theology beyond gender perspectives. To that group we need to add the number of men who are questioning heterosexuality in their theologies. The first generation of feminists still had a 'women this side, men the other side' approach which is not the case any more. If we are divided in our options and prejudices, it is more complex than that. Ideological stands go beyond gender classifications: gay theologians are also men.

Is queer the new feminism then? Yes and no. Somehow the old labels do not seem to work any more. Queer theologians stand for many of the same issues as feminist theologians, but they also have a different agenda based on their own experiences of how the sexual construction of religion and society have alienated their lives. Curiously at this point we are confronted by the fact that what is in crisis is not the movement called 'feminist theology' but rather the nomenclature. Something similar happened with the liberation theological movement. Its nomenclature may be in crisis, but not the struggle for peace and justice that still mobilizes so many theologians and church people in a continuous praxis of action and reflection. Moreover, the fact that the feminist theological disciplinary borders and critical framework have expanded proves only its growth, not its demise. Further, the situations of women around the globe alert us to the fact that feminist concerns are not over, all the ills have not been addressed and all the dreams not realized. So perhaps the queer agenda is the way ahead but for many this will be perceived as too radical a move – they will literally be frightened by what they believe the label means and stands for. Of course for some the 'F' word has always been frightening, while for others it continues to signal hope and change, both with the lives and aspirations of women in central stage. The list of concerns and injustices as well as aspirations and grand visions that needs to be carried by any word is ever-expanding as we realize the extreme complexity of what at first appeared a simple vision – the acknowledgement of the full humanity of women. This complexity may call for a range of words and theoretical approaches but we hope that the vision of a world that glories in the full humanity of women will not be lost through fragmentation and suspicion. Feminist theology has always been a multidisciplinary praxis and needs more than ever to remain true to that courage – make no mistake it takes considerable courage and insight to hold such a theoretical vision and our foresisters have left us a grand heritage.

The affirmation of the paradigm of difference in feminist theology still needs to allow for the challenging of discrimination, especially within ecclesiastical institutions. The positive recognition of difference stands in contrast to that negative noting of difference which is the basis of the legitimation and perpetuation of discrimination against women,[5] excluding them from leadership roles, positions of decision-making, or in some cases ordination. Of course it is open to feminist theologians to object to practices like ordination as such, viewing them as inherently oppressive. They may seek ecclesial structures which, being non-patriarchal, foster different forms of spirituality and pastoral care. Feminism is, after all, a distinctive way of relating, much more democratic and participative and less pre-occupied with hierarchical and authoritarian patterns. At the same time, not all societies have legal systems ensuring women equal pay for equal work, or welfare provision for mothers with young children. A contrast is sometimes made between feminist theologians working in socioeconomic contexts, addressing what are regarded as the 'real issues' facing women in their struggles, and feminist theologians working in theoretical elaborations. This is a false dichotomy which may indeed arise through the continuation of certain assumptions inherited from patriarchal thinking. As a way of illustrating this point, I recall how some years ago I found myself involved with other women developing a project to work with women in El Salvador. We had planned to carry out interviews and research in situ, and to produce a collective theological reflection on

---

5 For the 'equality' vs 'difference' shifts in feminist theory see, for instance, Judith Evans, *Feminist Theory Today: An Introduction to the Second Wave Feminism*, London: Sage, 1995, p. 146.

the situation of women after the war in El Salvador. One of the members of the team proposed that we should seek an opinion on the project from an eminent (male) liberation theologian from that country. It sounds contradictory but there is still a minority of women, in certain contexts, who welcome the authoritative advice of male theologians for their work. In this case, the answer from the liberation theologian was that the project was worthy, provided we accept one prerequisite: we should try to convey women's words as faithfully as possible, without adding anything to them, including theological reflections. That is, his advice was that no theological reflection should be allowed to take over the authenticity of women's thoughts and shared experiences. This counsel came from a man who belonged to a generation that consistently added theological reflection to the experiences of poor people. This was done confidently and routinely even though they had little in common with the people about whom they wrote. They offered solidarity and compassion but they had little in common with poor people, not social or economic status, not even nationality. They did not necessarily distort the experiences of the people, but they freely elaborated theologically upon them.

Two Brazilian theologians, the Boff brothers (Leonardo and Clodovis), for instance, went as far as to claim that there were different levels at which liberation theology could be done: some superficial and spontaneous, as in the case of popular theologies, and others deeper and more reflective, such as the work of professional theologians working on the experiences of the people.[6] What we have here is the idea that theologizing is not a proper activity for women. As a result, some feminist theologians of the developing world have suffered the consequences of a false dichotomy of 'intellectual versus practical', a binary category which could also have been formulated as 'nature versus culture' or 'caring versus thinking'. Such women theologians have been stereotyped as 'practical'

---

6 Cf. Leonardo and Clodovis Boff, *Introducing Liberation Theology*, New York: Orbis, 1987.

or 'experiential' women. One issue to consider for the future is the overcoming of these colonial, gendered intellectual traditions. Women, whether from the developing world, or the North Atlantic, whether from Asia, Africa or Latin America, must be recognized as genuine intellectual workers.

Feminist theology and its language

Many feminist theological conferences have witnessed debates on 'academic versus popular' language, ignited by the presentation of a paper using terminology which has not been understood, or covering themes which have been considered irrelevant to the lives of women outside academic circles. These situations usually arise when there has been a mismatch of experiences between the academic speaker and the audience. The whole paper is then considered irrelevant or full of jargon. This, in turn, provokes a discussion as to how much academic background is required of ordinary women even to understand the feminist theological language, a debate which can get out of hand. I was once present at a conference where such a discussion began from a question formulated by a woman as follows: 'Why do feminist theologians not write things that I can understand?' The issue at the heart of this controversy cannot be ignored and it might be useful to consider it when reflecting on the thinking of the future of feminist theologies. There are several possible responses to such a question. First of all, feminist theology is a discipline and like any other discipline requires training and study over a period of years. When Caddy Stanton wrote *The Women's Bible* in 1898, she advocated the study of Hebrew for women who wanted to read the scriptures from a women's perspective. Women in the nineteenth century understood that producing a women's theology required not only their experiences, but the right analytical tools. Today feminist theologians have expertise in biblical languages and in many critical frameworks of analysis, from ethnocentric methodologies and gender studies to postcolonialism theory, from psychology and sociology to continental philosophy. The list is extensive and the combination of perspectives is indeed the reason for the richness of our reflections. What we should celebrate is the fact that there are new, challenging fields of knowledge to investigate: something that is demanding for us to understand may be the source of changes in our lives. Some women may argue that precisely the practical nature of feminist theology lies at the core of the intellectual demand of our task.

Do we have, then, a confrontation between intellectuals and practicals? In both groups, if indeed such exist, the goal may be the same, but working with ideas is as important as going to public demonstrations. In fact, both things are closely related. We may be at risk of perpetuating the 'men as intellectuals' versus 'women as practical' dichotomies, and silencing the wealth of questioning still to be posited by feminist theologians. But can feminist theologians use 'plain speech'? Even Mary Daly, a radical theologian and philosopher, found as early as the 1970s that she needed to invent new words and concepts.[7] Women have not inherited a tradition of doing theology: they need to recreate it. They need sometimes to desystematize theology, to rethink doctrines and orthopraxis. They need to come with new reading and writing techniques, more faithful to what could be the real meaning of women thinking/reading/writing theology, the theological equivalent to the French *écriture féminine*.[8] There are levels of complexity, but not necessarily of vanity, involved here.

However, what this controversy illuminates is the fact that feminist theology needs to be part of a movement. If the movement ceases to exist we stop mobilizing ourselves to produce acts of social transformation. A feminist theological essay on motherhood needs to be accompanied by a demand, for instance, that universities

---

7 See Mary Daly and Jane Caputi (eds), *Webster's First New Intergalactic Wickedary of the English Language*, Boston: Beacon Press, 1987.

8 *Écriture féminine* (lit., 'women's writing' is part of a project developed by French feminists such as Hélène Cixous, Luce Irigaray, Julia Kristeva and Catherine Clément. It challenges male conventions and strategies in writing.

should have free nurseries for students' children. The fact that feminist academics may be perceived as remote from common life by other women is part of an old myth of academia and privileges – the reality today is very different. Women theologians are specialized workers. If they do not have time to engage in extra social and practical activities beyond the eight or ten hours they must work each day, that is because the structures and demands of educational systems need to be revised. Along with demands for working hours to be more humane, we also need to make sure that our networks are strong. Feminist theology remains a praxis-based theology and as such needs to maintain unique and challenging links between theory and praxis. There are gatherings in which this happens and they are to be supported and aided if the unique method that is feminist theology is to carry through many of the promises it shows.

Ruth Page, a Scottish theologian who has never been a feminist but has participated in feminist theology conferences, once declared that feminist theology should voluntarily decide to cease to exist, in order to be integrated into 'real theology'.[9] Her argument follows a classical, patriarchal line of thought, that the part must eventually be integrated into the sum total. She claims that as feminists have made their point, now it is time to leave gender aside and deal with the real issues of systematic theology. That is to say, for Page, feminist theology was a gender issue which needed to be incorporated and subsumed by the more proper line of argumentation and thinking presented by classical systematic theology. It goes without saying that this suggestion was never taken up. It was Page's own position and it has not provoked any discussion. Instead, in the past few years there has been a movement to view issues of gender as part of a larger agenda of justice. For some, gender issues belong together with matters of economic and racial justice; for others, gender issues, or issues of sexual justice, should be prioritized. And for yet

---

9 Cf. Ruth Page's article, 'Has Feminist Theology a Viable Long-Term Future?', in Deborah Sawyer and Diane Collier (eds), *Is There a Future for Feminist Theology?* Sheffield: Sheffield Academic Press, 1999, pp. 193–8.

others, an increasing group of theologians, gender and sexuality are seen as constituting the core of the theological enterprise. At heart it is not just an issue of equality and justice, but a whole epistemology responsible for a network of oppressive elements in the discourse of the sacred.

At the heart of this discourse of the sacred remains the big question of metaphysics and the problem which at their worst they have caused feminist theory and ideas of autonomy. The question of metaphysics is one that covers not only issues of transcendence and immanence, which have an impact on theological concerns such as the environment, but at root is a question of power. From the beginning feminist theologians have preferred to talk of empowerment and in that way have not always grasped the central question at the heart of any metaphysical system, that of power. This debate will carry on for a long time yet and we will have to see what the world looks like when we each take the power of our birthright, the *dunamis* that lives in us all.

The future of feminist theologies are assured while gender and sexual oppression exists. It is not only people who suffer but whole communities and even the earth. Environmental crimes are also gendered and there is a long tradition already of studies of the relationship between the patriarchal anthropology of the Bible and the attitudes of humanity towards nature. However, it is going to be a diverse future. As feminist theologians continue their search for ways of disentangling patriarchal ideology from theology, new issues concerning identity, ethics, methods and understandings of Christianity also evolve. There is not just one feminist theology project, but many, and they all have something to contribute to each other. Diversity and plurality, and on occasion even confrontation, are the strength of a theological movement which far from being passé still has much to contribute to the way we understand our Christian faith in the world today.

Bibliography

Althaus-Reid, M., *Indecent Theology: Theological Perversions in Sex, Gender and Politics*, London, Routledge, 2001.

Anson, J., 'The Female Transvestite in Early Monasticism: The Origin and Development of a Motif', *Viator*, Vol. 5, 1974.

Badham, P., *Christian Beliefs About Life After Death*, London, MacMillan, 1976.

Balasuriya, T., *Mary and Human Liberation: The Story and the Text*, London, Mowbray, 1997.

Bartky, S. L., *Femininity and Domination*, New York, Routledge, 1990.

Bingemer, M. C., 'Women in the Future of Liberation Theology' in M. Ellis and O. Maduro (eds), *The Future of Liberation Theology: Essays in Honour of Gustavo Gutiérrez*, New York, Orbis, 1989.

Boff, L. and C., *Introducing Liberation Theology*, New York, Orbis, 1987.

Borreson, K., *The Image of God*, Minneapolis, Fortress Press, 1995.

Braidotti, R., *Nomadic Subjects: Embodiment and Sexual Difference in Contemporary Feminist Theory*, New York, Columbia University Press, 1994.

Brock, R., *Journeys by Heart: A Christology of Erotic Power*, New York, Crossroad, 1988.

Butler, J., *Gender Trouble: Feminism and the Subversion of Gender*, London, Routledge, 1990.

Butler, J., *The Psychic Life of Power*, California, Stanford University Press, 1997.

Butler, J., *Undoing Gender*, London, Routledge, 2004.

Christ, C., 'Why Women Need the Goddess' in the journal *Heresies: The Great Goddess Issue* (1978), reprinted in C. Christ and J. Plaskow (eds),

Womanspirit Rising: A Feminist Reader on Religion, San Francisco, Harper and Row, 1979.

Christ, C., *Laughter of Aphrodite: Reflections on a Journey to the Goddess*, San Francisco, Harper and Row, 1987.

Chung Hyun Kyung, *Struggle to Be the Sun Again: Introducing Asian Women's Theology*, London, SCM Press, 1990.

Chung Hyun Kyung, *Goddess-Spell According to Hyung Kyung: A Letter from Goddess to the Earth and Keeping Women Warriors of the World*, Pa-Yu, Yolimwon, 2001.

Conner, R., *Queering Creole Spiritual Traditions*, New York, Harrington Park Press, 2004.

Daly, M., *Gyn/Ecology: The Metaethics of Radical Feminism*, Boston, Beacon Press, 1990.

Daly, M., *Beyond God the Father*, Boston, Beacon Press, 1993.

Daly, M. and Caputi, J. (eds), *Webster's First New Intergalactic Wickedary of the English Language*, Boston, Beacon Press, 1987.

Davison, P., 'Obituary: *Comandante Ramona*' (9 January 2006), available online: http://news.independent.co.uk/people/obituaries/article337439. ece.

Doresse, J., *The Secret Books of the Egyptian Gnostics: An Introduction to the Gnostic Coptic Manuscripts Discovered at Chenoboskion with an English translation and Critical Evaluation of the Gospel of Thomas*, New York, Harper, 1960.

Dussel, E. (ed.), *La Iglesia en Latinoamérica 1492–1992*, New York, Orbis, 1992.

Elizondo, V., *La Morenita: Evangelizer of the Americas*, San Antonio, TX, Mexican American Cultural Centre Press, 1980.

Evans, J., *Feminist Theory Today: An Introduction to the Second Wave Feminism*, London, Sage, 1995.

Gebara, I. and Bingemer, M. C., *Mary: Mother of God, Mother of the Poor*, New York, Orbis, 1989.

Goldenberg, N., *Changing the Gods: Feminism and the End of Traditional Religion*, Boston, Beacon Press, 1979.

Grey, M., *Redeeming the Dream: Feminism, Redemption and Christian Tradition*, London, SPCK, 1989.

Grey, M., *Sacred Longings: Ecofeminist Theology and Globalisation*, London, SCM Press, 2003.

Grey, M., *The Unheard Scream: The Struggles of Dalit Women in India*, New Dehli, Centre for Dalit/Subaltern Studies, 2004.

Gross, R., 'Where Have We Been? Where Do We Need to Go?: Women's Studies and Gender in Religion and Feminist Theology', in U. King and T. Beattie (eds), *Gender, Religion and Diversity: Cross Cultural Perspectives*, London, Continuum, 2004.

Gudorf, C. quoted in E. Schussler Fiorenza and S. Copeland, *Violence Against Women*, London, Concilium, 1994.

Halperin, D. M., *Saint Foucault: Towards a Gay Hagiography*, Oxford, Oxford University Press, 1995.

Hampson, D., *Theology and Feminism*, Oxford, Blackwell, 1990.

Hampson, D., *After Christianity*, London, SCM Press, 1996.

Hampson, D., *Swallowing a Fishbone*, London, SPCK, 1996.

Heyward, C., *The Redemption of God*, Lanham, University of America Press, 1982.

Howson, A., *Embodying Gender*, London, Sage, 2005.

Isherwood, L., *Liberating Christ*, Cleveland, OH, Pilgrim Press, 1999.

Isherwood, L. (ed.), *The Good News of the Body: Sexual Theology and Feminism*, Sheffield, Sheffield Academic Press, 2000.

Isherwood, L., 'Indecent Theology: What F…ing Difference Does it Make?', *Feminist Theology*, Vol. 11.2 (January 2003).

Isherwood, L., *The Power of Erotic Celibacy: Queering Heteropatriarchy*, London, T&T Clark, 2006.

Isherwood, L., 'Jesus Past the Posts', in L. Isherwood and K. McPhillips, *Post Christian Feminisms*, London, Ashgate, 2007.

Isherwood, L., '"Eat, Friends, Drink. Be Drunk with Love" (Song of Songs 5.2). A Reflection', in L. Isherwood (ed.), *Patriarchs, Prophets and Other Villains*, London, Equinox, forthcoming.

Jantzen, G., *Power, Gender and Christian Mysticism*, Cambridge, Cambridge University Press, 1995.

Jantzen, G., 'Sources of Religious Knowledge', *Literature and Theology*, Vol. 10.2 (June 1996).

Johnson, E., 'Redeeming the Name of Christ', in C. M. LaCugna (ed.),

Freeing Theology: The Essentials of Theology in Feminist Perspective, New York, Harper, 1993.

Kee, A., *The Rise and Demise of Black Theology*, London, Ashgate, 2006.

Keller, C., *Apocalypse Now and Then*, Boston, Beacon Press, 1996.

Kwok Pui-Lan, 'Jesus the Native', in F. F. Segovia and M. A. Tolbert (eds), *Teaching the Bible: The Discourse and Politics of Biblical Pedagogy*, Maryknoll, Orbis, 1998.

Kwok Pui-Lan, *Postcolonial Imagination and Feminist Theology*, Westminster, John Knox Press, 2005.

Lennon, K. and Whitford, M., *Knowing the Difference: Feminist Perspectives in Epistemology*, London, Routledge, 1994.

Lorde, A., *Sister Outsider*, California, Crossing Press, 1984.

McDannell, C. and Lang, B., *Heaven: A History*, London, Yale University Press, 1988.

Martin, J. G., 'Liberating Palestinian Theology – The Need for a Contextual Spirituality', in U. King (ed.), *Spirituality and Society in the New Millennium*, Brighton, Sussex Academic Press, 2001.

Melancton, M., 'Christology and Women', in V. Fabella and Sun Ai Lee Park, *We Dare to Dream: Doing Theology as Asian Women*, Hong Kong, AWRCCT, 1989.

Oduyoye, M., *Daughters of Anowa: African Women and Patriarchy*, New York, Orbis, 1995.

Page, R., 'Has Feminist Theology a Viable Long-Term Future?', in D. Sawyer and D. Collier (eds), *Is There a Future for Feminist Theology?*, Sheffield, Sheffield Academic Press, 1999.

Porcile Santiso, M. T., *La Mujer: Espacio de Salvación*, Perú, Trilce, 1991.

Ricciardi, R. and Hurault, B., *El Nuevo Testamento: La Biblia Latinoamericana*, Madrid, Verbo Divino, 1972.

Ruether, R. R., 'Motherearth and the Megamachine: A Theology of Liberation in a Feminine, Somatic and Ecological Perspective', in C. Christ and J. Plaskow (eds), *Womanspirit Rising: A Feminist Reader on Religion*, San Francisco, Harper & Row, 1979.

Ruether, R. R., 'Ecofeminism and Healing Ourselves, Healing the Earth', *Feminist Theology*, Vol. 9, Sheffield, Sheffield Academic Press, 1995, pp. 51–62.

Ruether, R. R., *Introducing Redemption in Christian Feminism*, Sheffield, Sheffield Academic Press, 1998.

Ruether, R. R. in Panel III: Feminist Theology II, Religion and the Feminist Movement Conference at Harvard Divinity School, November 2002. (http://www.hds.harvard.edu/wsrp/scholarhip/rfmc/rfm_video.html).

Ruether, R. R., *Goddesses and the Divine Feminine: A Western Religious History*, Berkeley, University of California Press, 2005.

Schüssler Fiorenza, E., *Jesus: Miriam's Child, Sophia's Prophet: Critical Issues in Feminist Christologies*, London, Continuum, 1995.

Schüssler Fiorenza, E., *Wisdom Ways: Introducing Feminist Biblical Interpretation*, New York, Orbis, 2001.

Southard, N. F., 'Recovery and Rediscovered Images: Spiritual Resources for Asian American Women', in U. King, *Feminist Theology from the Third World*, London, SPCK, 1994.

Stuart, E., 'Elizabeth Stuart Phelps: A Good Woman Doing Bad Theology', *Feminist Theology*, Vol. 26, Sheffield, Sheffield Academic Press, 2001.

Stuart, E., 'Exploding Mystery: Feminist Theology and the Sacramental', *Feminist Theology*, Vol. 12.2, London, Continuum, 2004.

Támez, E., 'Introduction: The Power of the Naked', in E. Támez (ed.), *Through Her Eyes: Women's Theology from Latin America*, New York, Orbis, 1989.

Tessier, T., *Dancing After the Whirlwind*, Boston, Beacon Press, 1997.

Trible, P., *Texts of Terror: Literary-Feminist Readings of Biblical Narratives*, Minneapolis, Ausburg Fortress Publishers, 1984.

Von Kellenbach, K., 'Overcoming the Teaching of Contempt', in A. Brenner and C. Fontaine (eds), *A Feminist Companion to Reading the Bible: Approaches, Methods and Strategies*, Sheffield, Sheffield Academic Press, 1997.

Vuola, E., *Limits of Liberation: Feminist Theology and the Ethics of Poverty and Reproduction*, London, Continuum, 2002.

Vuola, E., 'Seriously Harmful for Your Health? Religion, Feminism and Sexuality in Latin America', in M. Althaus-Reid (ed.), *Liberation Theology and Sexuality*, London, Ashgate, 2006.

Walker, A., *In Search of Our Mothers' Gardens*, London, The Women's Press, 1994.

Walker Bynum, C., *The Resurrection of the Body in Western Christianity, 200–1336*, New York, Columbia University Press, 1995.

Williams, D., 'Black Women's Surrogate Experience and the Christian Notion of Redemption', in W. Eakin, J. B. McDaniel and P. Cooey (eds), *After Patriarchy: Feminist Transformations of the World Religions*, New York, Orbis, 1991.

Williams, D., *Sisters in the Wilderness: The Challenge of Womanist God-Talk*, New York, Orbis, 1993.

Index of Names and Subjects

Aboriginal Jesus 103–4
Afro Brazilian Cults 67, 75
Althaus-Reid, Marcella 3, 4,
  44, 76, 81, 103–4, 144, 148
Ambrose 19
Anson, John 20, 136
Aquino, Maria Pilar 38, 43
Asian theologies 41, 49, 63, 72,
  83, 87, 136, 139
  and identity 46, 88, 127
  and Bible 54
Augustine 112–3, 121

Badham, Paul 112, 136
Balasuriya, Tissa 72
Black Madonna 75
Bartky, Sandra Lee 18
Bible 6, 49, 52–4, 58, 132
  and interreligious
    hermeneutics 55, 60
  and the Virgin Mary 69, 72–3,
    79
  and Sophia 100
  and Queer hermeneutics 78
  and Postcolonialism 44, 62,
    103–4

Bingemer, Maria Clara 68, 71,
  136–7
Biological determinism 84
Bisexual theology 20, 127–8
Black American theology 13,
  39, 40, 86
Boff, Leonardo and Clodovis
  72, 131
Borresen, Kari 19
Braidotti, Rosi 25, 26, 136
British and Irish School of
  Feminist Theology 11
Brock, Rita N. 30–1, 91, 136
Buddhism 35
Butler, Judith 2, 22, 25,
  28–9, 136
Bynum, Walker 113–4, 140

Caddy Stanton, Elizabeth 132
Carter Heyward, I 30, 32, 92–3
Central American theologians
  7
Christ, Carol 50
Christology 64, 90, 92, 70,
  81–87, 97
  and sin and salvation 91, 92

and the erotic 94
and Queer theologies 95–6
and Sophia 98–101
see also Judaism; resurrection
(Chung) Hyung Kyung 49, 50,
   66, 88 136–7
Church Fathers 22
Circle of Concerned African
   Theologians 126
Comandante Ramona 79
Conner, Randy 126

Dalit Theology 127
Daly, Mary 1, 27, 52, 65, 77, 82,
   133
Death 114–24
Diaspora of women theologians
   8, 45
Doresse, Jean 20
Dualistic thinking 13–4, 93, 96,
   100, 103, 106, 114–5, 122, 124
Dube, Muse 44, 126
Dussel, Enrique 67

Ecclesial structures 61, 130
Ecofeminism 117–8
Elizondo, Virgilio 67
Empowerment 5, 13, 24
Erotic Celibacy 29, 35
Ethics 65–6, 74, 135
Evans, Judith 130

Fabella, Virginia 83
Fathers of the Church 19–23,
   32, 111–2

Feminism 4, 9–10, 21, 25–6,
   49–52, 65, 69, 73, 76, 82, 89,
   97, 117–8, 125, 128–9
Feminist hermeneutics 12, 38,
   41–3
   and culture 44–5, 50, 55, 57,
   127, 130
Feminist Theologies 41, 46–7.
   49, 56, 60, 64, 85, 96, 106–7,
   123–8, 132, 135
Filipino women doing theology
   82, 94
   and Mariology 63–4, 78, 84
Foucault, Michel 22–3
Freud, Sigmund 23–4

Gebara, Yvonne 68
Gender 3, 10, 14, 18–21
   and culture 6
   and sexual identity 7, 9, 12, 17
   and Queer theory 15
Genesis 18–9, 57
Goddess 40–51, 59, 67, 70–1,
   75, 77, 87, 102, 127
Goldenberg, Naomi 50
Good Sex project 35
Gospel of Thomas 20
Goss, Robert 9
Grey, Mary 3, 72, 89, 92, 127
Gross, Rita 126
Gudorf, Christine 87

Halperin, David 23
Hampson, Daphne 3, 52, 65,
   77

Hanks, Thomas 9
Harrison, Beverley 33
Hebrew Scriptures 18, 70, 98,
    102, 107
Heterosexuality 51, 69, 127–9,
    79, 95
Hildegard of Bingen 114–6,
    118, 120
Holy Spirit 15, 66
Homogeneization in theology
    6, 15
and sexual identity 39, 126
Howson, Alexandra 24

Identity 9–12, 25, 27, 38–41, 48,
    52, 61–2, 109, 123, 135
and sexuality 7–8
and hermeneutics 53–55, 60
and Mariology 13, 64–5, 78
and discrepancies 45–6
Iemanjá 75
Incarnational theology 101, 113
Indecent Theology 36–7, 58,
    68, 73, 95–6
Intifada 55
Irigaray, Luce 24, 26, 133
Isasi-Díaz, Ada Maria 38, 47
Isherwood, Lisa 21, 29, 32, 35,
    37, 84, 97, 116, *see also* Erotic
    Celibacy

Jantzen, Grace 53, 118
Jeffreys, Sheila 34–5
Jerome 19
Jesus the native 103–4

Jesus' movement 29, 97–8, 110
Job 107
Johnson, Elizabeth 99, 100
Jouissance 24
Judaism 51, 72, 81, 97–8, 101–3
Justice 17, 27, 53, 61, 64, 90–1,
    122
and embodiment 2, 37, 113,
    125
and sexuality 4, 9, 134–5

Kanyoro, Musimbi 59
Kee, Alistair 40
Keller, Catherine 117
King, Ursula 55, 87, 126
Korean women theology 49,
    88
Kuan Ying 87–8
Kwok Pui Lan 44, 54, 103–4,
    126

La realidad 43
Lacan, Jacques 22–5
Latin American Bible 66
Latin American theologies
    Latina theology 7, 38–9,
    43–6, 62, 127
Lennon, Kathleen 23
Liberation theology 36, 54, 58,
    64, 71–3, 78, 95, 115, 131
Liturgy 5, 56, 121–2
Lo cotidiano 43
Lorde, Audre 27, 30
Love 31, 37, 88–9, 93–5, 100,
    116

McPhillips, Kath 97

Marianismo 63, 73

Mariology of Liberation 68, 73, 78, *see also* Virgin Mary; Marianismo

Mark's Gospel 32

Martin, Judith 55

Maya Tzotzil 78–9

Melancton, Monica 83

Melano Couch, Beatriz 47

Mesters, Carlos 58

Methodologies 1, 6–7, 15, 26, 33, 38, 41, 44, 47, 69, 126, 128, 132

Ming Jung women 61

Mollenkott, Virginia 47

Montanism 21

Musskopft, André 9

Neo-Platonism 81

Non-metaphysical Christ 97

Normativity 23, 59

Oduyoye, Mercy 49

Otherness 26

Page, Ruth 134

Palestinian women and theology 55

Patriarchy 4–5, 8, 22, 26, 32, 49, 51, 102, 121–2

Philo of Alexandria 109

Plaskow, Judith 47, 50, 82

Politics and feminist theologies 43–45, 49, 78, 90

Porcile Santiso, Maria Teresa 63–4, 76

Postfeminism 9

Postmodernism 14, 34, 79, 105, 128

Power and structures of oppression 10, 15–6, 128

and gender 26, 30–1

and resistance 23

Praxis 6–9, 18, 41–2, 49, 55, 58–60, 129–30, 133–4

and redemption 89, 116

Prisca and Maximilla 21

Queer Mary 77–9

Queer theology 9, 13–4, 36, 58, 121, 126, 128

Queer theory 3, 13, 15, 34, 62, 69, 129

Race, gender and sexuality 21, 37, 39–40, 46, 127–8

and different contexts 13, 39–40, 46, 127–8

and the Virgin Mary 75

Radford Ruether, Rosemary 6, 42–3, 47, 59, 70–2, 81–4, 90–2, 102, 117–9, 120, 125

Ratzinger, Joseph 121

Redemption 32, 82, 84, 89, 90–4, 111, 120

S & M (Sadomasochism) 23, 35

Salvation 19, 89–92, 100, 123–4

Secular society 18
Sexual suspicion 51
Sheol 107–9
Sisterhood 1, 27, 85
Sophia 70, 98–101
Spirituality 30, 51,–2, 55, 63,
   70–3, 77–8, 89, 117, 130
Southard, Naomi 87
Stuart Phelps, Elizabeth 119–21
Stuart, Elizabeth 5, 119–22
Sun Ai Lee Park 83
Symbols 22–5, 43, 48–50, 75

Támez, Elsa 49
Thecla 19–21
Tessier, Tess 30
Thealogy 50, 77, 126, *see also*
   Goddess
Transsexuality 21, 34, 128
Transvestitism 20, *see also*
   Thecla
Trible, Phyllis 52

United Nations and Gay Rights
   28

Vatican 28

Virgin Mary 7, 13, 56–7, 63–72,
   75, 77–9
Virgin of Copacabana 75
Virgin of Dietrich 78
Virgin of Guadalupe 78, 63,
   67, 79
Von Kellenbach, Katharina 101
Vuola, Elina 63, 73–4, 76

Walker, Alice 40
Western thought and feminism
   2, 4–10, 22, 35, 79, 91, 94,
   103–4, 115, 119, 122–3
Whitefeminists 125
Whitford, Margaret 23
Williams, Delores 43, 47, 49,
   85–6
Womanists 7, 39, 49, 86, 88, 127
Women's Church 56, 60
Women's ordination 7, 12, 15,
   61, 71–2, 125, 130

Xena, Warrior Princess 95

Zapatistas 78, *see also*
   Comandante Ramona
Zoroastrian religion 108